The Witch Doctor and The Man

City Under the Sea

Pat Holliday, Ph.D.

and

Bishop Samuel Vagalas Kanco

Printed in the United States of America.

All Scripture quotations are taken from the
King James Version of the Bible

ISBN: 978-1-884785-01-6

Agapepublishers
9252 San Jose Blvd, #2804
Jacksonville , Florida 32257
904-733-8318

This book is affectionately dedicated with grateful thanks to my beloved wife, Reverend Evelyn Kanco, my constant encourager and prayer warrior.

Preface

And though they hide themselves in the top of Carmel, I will search and take them out thence; and though they be hid from my sight in the bottom of the sea, thence will I command the serpent, and he shall bite them. (Amos 9:3)

This book was not written to promote the powers of the Devil. Truly, it has been published to reveal the sovereign power of God and His ability to save and free the strongest captives of Satan. The scripture says, "For God sent not his Son into the world to condemn the world, but that the world through him might be saved. He that believeth on him is not condemned; but he that believeth not is condemned already, because he hath not believed in the name of the only begotten Son of God," (John 3:17,18).

Bishop Kanco is a towering six-foot-six African with penetrating brown eyes that seem to see into your spirit. Indeed, he appeared mythological dressed in an African white gold accented outfit. He reminded me of a warrior ready for battle displaying tribal, jet-black scars across his cheeks. He is such an incredible man of God, I thought. He is a stately person with a splendid perceptual gift. These were my impressions the first time that I saw Bishop Vagalas Kanco.

His presence is genuine. The most dominant feature that I noticed was his deep concentrated fixed gaze that seemed able to see into the center of a person's being. There were great mysteries deep within his spirit. However, the most phenomenal characteristic is his supernatural sensitivity. Truly, I have never met anyone like him. He merely tunes into you as though he has a spiritual radar system. When he fastens his X-ray eyes upon you, he appears to see everything.

When I arrived at the church that he was visiting in Florida, he was already ministering. After he finished his sermon, I walked up to him and said, "Hello, I'm Dr. Pat Holliday." His eyes sparkled and replied as though he recognized me. "I know."

When he smiled, I felt as though I was under a spiritual microscope and was taken aback, to say the least. I extended my hand. He took it into his giant hand, having a mystifying look on his face. "I have a ..." However, before I could finish the sentence, he finished it for me, "a miracle ministry."

"But I also have ..."

He broke in again and finished the sentence, "a deliverance ministry."

"On the other hand, I also have a ..."

Bishop Vagalas interrupted me again, "a teaching ministry," he exclaimed!

Warmly he said, "My name is Vagalas Kanco from Ghana, West Africa and I want you to come to Africa. I will host you there."

It was an incredible experience. I have never had a person to look into my spirit and discern me that clearly before. He seemed to know me by the Spirit of God and there was no question about it. My administrator, Dr. Sabrina Sessions, was taken a back also. Later she said, "Doctor Pat, can a man come three thousand miles, all the way from Africa, and know you like that by the Spirit. It's really remarkable because the people here still don't know you?"

"A person is never received in their hometown, Sabrina. The Bible says that His hometown people did not receive Jesus. Bishop Kanco is a spiritual man, and supernatural and he can hear from God."

Then I sincerely sought the Lord's will about going to Ghana. "Lord, if You want me to go, You would have to have that man call me."

One day, he called and asked, "When will you come to Africa?" I made an appointment to go in November.

The Lord spoke gently to my spirit, "Go, I will pay for it." He did and blessed me with some financial seed to sow while in Africa.

When my team arrived in Africa, we were met by some of the friendliest people in the world. They were dancing, singing and praising the Lord. I was amazed that the atmosphere was very peaceful in the city and shocked to see so many businesses with biblical names. I saw no one smoking or drinking on the streets of the city.

"We are in a great revival," Pastor Evelyn Kanco said.

It was such an incredible thing to see Bishop Kanco's church. It was packed out. There more than 10,000 members in the mother church plus the members of the 900 churches that he and his wife, and the ministers trained in their Bible school have planted; I was very amazed at the Bishop's ministry. The devils scream out and tremble at the sound of his voice. The spiritual atmosphere is charged with the power of the Holy Ghost in his church. Miracles, signs and wonders are common. The blind can see. The lame walk, and cancers are healed as easily as a cold. He ministered the first night that we were there; about twenty witches were spiritually manifesting apparent demonic possession by screaming and jerking.

When the Holy Spirit's anointing came, they fell out in their chairs. Then, the forty men and women that had been trained in the deliverance ministry by the Bishop met them. The spiritual war was on, and they were freed by the power of the name of Jesus. He most certainly has the spiritual anointing.

American churches need the message of deliverance. We have wonderful churches in our country, but many of our churches have become lukewarm, cold, materialistic, and religious while others, are self-centered. We must return to the basics of the Bible. I believe that God is calling Bishop Kanco to bring the message of the need for deliverance to our nation.

After witnessing his ministry in Africa, I was delighted that he asked me to help him to write his story. It is not every day that you meet someone with centuries of bloodlines of wizards that were serving idols. However, this book concerns his fourth generational line of witch doctors, many who have become born again. Also I have five brothers who are serving Jesus! What a powerful testimony!

His testimony is so needed today because the people in our nation have lost their fear of God or the Devil. Many Christians no longer believe in Satan's existence.

Bishop Kanco knows, and has experienced supernatural powers from both sides of the invisible world. He can be used by God to warn our people of its dangers while at the same time, clean the churches from religious bondages. I have many books to type that are written in my mind. However, I believe this book will be one of the most important testimonies that I will ever attempt to write I believe it will open the spiritual mind of the western church to see that we are missing a large part of Jesus Christ's teaching—setting the captives free! This part of Jesus' message that is not spooky but is vital for the survival of the church in such abounding darkness. It is the scriptural missing element needed to bring the kingdom of God to Americans and the world. Millions have walked into Satan's trap. Regrettably they can't find a way out.

When one has been ensnared by the powers of the Devil, you rarely see him get free in the modern Christian church. In short, it is a terrible thing to see someone under subjection to the powers of darkness. Only a broken, passionate church will attempt to free those who are in bondage. Yes, Satan is alive and well on the great planet earth, but so is our Jesus.

While Satan has used agents to capture the souls of men, women and children in our nation, Jesus has Saints like Bishop Kanco committed to free the captives. Bishop Kanco is such a Saint for such a time as this. To God is the glory forevermore!

Pat Holliday, Ph.D.
http://www.patholliday.com
http://www.miracleinternetchurch.com

Contents

Part 1:

City Under the Sea

Chapter One

Spiritual Roots

I am the Lord thy God...Thou shalt have no other gods before me. Thou shalt not make unto thee any graven image...(Exodus 20:2-4)

I am Bishop Samuel Vagalas Kanco of the Lord's Vineyard International Ministries, a wonderful Christian church, located in Accra, Ghana, West Africa. Jesus Christ is my personal Savior. I am blessed to be the first person that Jesus called out of witchcraft practiced in my family to become a child of God. Jesus commissioned me to "go and tell My people what I have done for you."

My testimony concerns the Lord's mercy, grace and deliverance. It is also a confirmation that there is no sin that His blood cannot wash away to make a person's spirit as white as snow. My story is one of hope for the billions of people that wish to be delivered by Jesus who are ensnared and made captive by idolatry and from family witchcraft ties. My country's religion is based on a mixture of the worship of idols and ancestors. My family worshiped idols such as gods of sun, moon, earth, trees, monkeys, snakes, etc. These were the only gods that we knew.

MY FATHER'S SON

I was born on Thursday 1st January 1960, the first son of Aloriga Kanco. My father named me Vagalas Kanco. I want to talk about myself, how I met Jesus Christ and became born again. My testimony is about being delivered from fourth-generational witch doctor family spirits to become a child of God. I was born to a typical idolatrous home in Ghana, West Africa.

My family originally came to Ghana from Upper Volta. They named the village Vea after their god in Bolgantaga. I was raised as a bushman and still have the jet-black markings on my face from Frafra Tribal ritualism. This mark across my cheeks confirmed my rites of passage to manhood.

The scars were also Satan's marks of my spiritual inheritance as the eldest son.

I am not a stranger to demons because I was born to become the fourth generational witch doctor in my family. As the eldest son, I was supposed to inherit my father's witch doctor position and supernatural powers.

Thank God that Jesus saved me before this demonic mantle was passed to me. Nevertheless, my father was training me to step into his witch doctor's leadership.

My father had a good mind, but he had inherited a passionate and headstrong character from his mother. She had brought her children up to be strong believers in witchcraft. She also took a great interest in relatives and friends, remembering the children's birthdays and anniversaries and deaths. She'd walk a long way to visit people, even visiting them in hospitals. It seemed my father spent his life busy with his witchcraft and serving his people. I must say, that I share my grandmother's hardheaded stubbornness.

A CHOSEN VESSEL

When Jesus rescued me out of the clutches of Satan, I had been a wizard for 12 years. Even so, God had other plans for my life. He chose me. He supernaturally saved, delivered, trained and called me. He wants to use my background to reveal to His church the mysteries of the majestic authority over Satan's schemes and the power of deliverance. The Bible shows that each one of us must find Jesus Christ as personal Savior. I was actually translated from the kingdom of darkness and placed into the Kingdom of God. God made me a new spiritual being. Before receiving Jesus, my spirit was dead to God. I was governed through my soul (mind) and my flesh before being born again. After being saved, I became spiritually alive to become a son of God to be led by His Holy Spirit.

Satan controls all pagan religions! It doesn't matter if it's the worship of Pan, Krishna, Diana or Thor. The faces behind the mask of these gods belong to Satan. Even if a person is an atheist, or whether it's the idol of power, money, knowledge, or some other ideal, still Satan is being worshiped.

The true God says,

> I am the Lord thy God...Thou shalt have no other gods before me. Thou shalt not make unto thee any graven image (idol), or any likeness of anything that is in heaven above, or that is in the earth beneath, or that is in the water under the earth: Thou shalt not bow down thyself to them, nor serve them: for I the Lord thy God am a jealous God... (Exodus 20:2–5)

It's that simple. There are two religious systems in the world. Satan controls one. The other owes its allegiance only to Jesus Christ. Put simply, if a person is not a believer in Jesus as Almighty God, incarnate Jesus that came in the flesh to save him from his sins, he belongs to Satan.

To sum up, the Bible shows that when Satan tempted Adam and Eve, they sinned (or fell) from a spiritual walk with God; since that time, every person on earth is born under the curse of darkness. Jesus Christ redeems mankind and restores them to the Father. Therefore, my Savior, Jesus, returned me to the same original spiritual condition that Adam and Eve enjoyed before their fall into sin. So, I don't wear wizards' robes anymore.

I have been washed in the blood of Jesus. Today, I stand in a glistening white robe awaiting His return. This is my testimony that I have written for His glory.

Chapter Two

Fourth Generation Witch Doctor

Thou shalt not bow down thyself to them, [worship them] nor serve them: for I the Lord thy God am a jealous God, visiting the iniquity of the fathers upon the children unto the third and fourth generation of them that hate me; And showing mercy unto thousands of them that love me, and keep my commandments. (Exodus 20:5–6)

FAMILY LIFE IN GHANA

Ghana is a beautiful place in which to grow up. My memory is filled with Africa's rich natural beauty. The country is almost completely surrounded by oceans and has many splendid lakes and rivers. The land is made up mainly of tropical rain forests, savannas, deserts, mountains, and waterfalls. The equator goes through Africa. Ghana and countries close to the equator have a tropical or hot climate.

My struggle started the day I was born into an idolatrous family in Africa. My village was small. Before I tell you about my unusual conversion to Christianity, I want to give a brief sketch of my own family and upbringing. My father was sincere about his witchcraft religion. He sat on a very powerful supernatural throne. The entire village would come to him. Even some Christians would come to seek his advice. Meanwhile my mother, Mary, assisted him in his witchcraft. However, she was happy to be a mother. She was content being with me to watch me grow. She took her wifely duties very seriously. Every day she prepared our meals in a small clay pot. I watched her closely each time she squatted to fire the tiny burner. She had just the right touch to kindle the flame for the fuel. A fond memory that I have was the special treat when she brought us finger bananas from the local plantations. There were few luxuries in our lives, but this is one of my outstanding memories from earlier childhood.

My mother suffered her lot without one complaining word. Her little thin body told the tale of the lack of nourishing foods. She enjoyed sons, but still, she was wife first, and mother second. She went about her duties with dull eyes, but they would sparkle each time she saw my brothers and me.

Nevertheless, an empty life is a fearful thing. Everything was so futile and nothing worth believing in, and gradually my heart grew more dark and confused. The people of an African village depend on each other as an extended family. In fact, it is not usual for everyone in a village to be related in one way or another. Traditionally the men are responsible for farming the land that surrounds the village. The women help with the farm work and they also cook and take care of the children. Villages very seldom have modern machines or tools for cooking or farming. Plowing is done with a wooden plow pulled by oxen. Food is prepared with the same kind of hand tool that has been used in Africa for hundreds of years. One traditional cooking tool found in nearly every West African home is the mortar and pestle.

A pestle is a club-shaped utensil used to pound food in the mortar. The most important "tool" used in traditional Africa is fire. Some West Africans still cook over a fire, just as our ancestors did.

Even the children have their role in the life of the village. At an early age, they learn to help the adults. They do whatever they can until they are old enough to take on adult responsibilities. My first household duty was collecting the fuel for our food. Barefooted, I had to travel about three miles each way. Collecting tiny twigs and thorny bushes, I squeezed them into small bundles. It was a humdrum job, but like every young boy, my mind managed to make it a major adventure each time that I had to make the trip to the forest. Centuries of famine, starvation and drought have taken their toll upon my people. It was a common thing to witness tragedies. For instance, I remember a young boy my own age who had a broken leg. His leg was being held together with two ounces of plaster of Paris and, without a doctor available, was clumsily and crookedly set.

For every poor African family, getting water was another major job. This was also one of my chores. Our water source was located about one mile from our hut. Everyone in the village came to the river for water. It was the only water supply for my entire community. Young and old, they came for this life's source of water. My jug was as large as those borne by older boys many years my senior. I could manage it just as easily as they could carry theirs. This job gave me a good chance to get to know the many people in the village. I saw the women with weary dullness in their eyes. No hope came from those eyes. They had no future. In fact, they had the very same look my mother and father had in their eyes…glossy, blank and dead.

The heat caused our body odors to mingle in the air. The people do not bathe every day. The ever-present armies of flies moved with a whirling motion, determined to land on our faces. No one was exempt from this unpleasant sensation, but not one person ever raised a hand to bat the flies away. I hated the gnats worst than the flies. They had a way of making themselves stick to the sweat on my skin. Their piercing stings caused itching bumps. Filling the water jug to the brim, I lifted the heavy container over my shoulder and rested it on my back and moved down the dusty roads like a beast of a burden.

It was always hot. The wind was always still. My hair was matted by the sweat of the day. It felt good to feel the cool water slush and spill a few drops down my hot back. Sometimes, I would jog especially hard to make it splash more. Always, before my father could inspect my jug and ask why it was not filled to the brim, I'd run to empty it into a larger bowl. This careless sloshing of hard-to-get water always caused me to make more trips to the river. However, it provided a small pleasure for me each time the water splashed on my hot back. Each time I had to take my journey to the village water source, I was joined by a swarming mass of humanity. I liked to see the large vultures fly in circles in the sky, while apple-green birds with long tapered beaks hopped about the hungry and thirsty people.

FAMILY BACKGROUND

I did not learn about witchcraft like some people because I was born into it. I grew up in that atmosphere of darkness. That is, my family worshiped idols. Likewise, they were witch doctors, witches, and wizards. Because we did not know God, whatever anyone can think about, we were involved in it. That is what we knew. As a result, my great-grandfather, my grandfather and father did not know anything about Jesus. They had never stepped into a church. Spiritually they were bound by the idol that they were serving.

It was my family duty to take care of the idols and their sacred food. Mmm, bananas, these were bigger and better than the ones that my mother brought home. Then I remember those juicy mangoes, rice and butter that all had the most distinctive mouth-watering flavors. Stark fear hit my heart the day my mother found me doing my favorite thing, eating the idol's food.

"Vagalas, what does you think you are doing," she challenged sharply, standing with her hands on her hips. When our eyes connected and locked, she gave me a long penetrating stare.

Her voice startled me. "I...uh...I was..."

My mind was speeding a thousand times a second. "I...uh...was testing the food for the welfare of the gods. I wanted to make sure the food was fresh!"

"Sure you are," she shook her head.

Trying to look regretful, "I'm sorry." She looked away quickly. I could see a soft-hidden smile behind her anger.

"See to it that you never do this again. It's dangerous! You must not anger the gods, they will never smile on you for many lives to come," she commanded. She was filled with disappointment. My family believed that the idol Vea was their savior. In order to become a priest to this idol, a man must go through many rituals. For example, a wizard cannot bathe for a year. Whenever he takes a bath, he cannot dry himself with a towel. In Africa, we have the bright sun, so a man can easily dry. Furthermore, wizards wear a white khaliko cloth and cannot sleep on a pillow. The devils will allow a wizard to sleep only a few minutes at a time. Actually, I was allowed to sleep two hours the entire night, and sometimes only thirty minutes. Satan is a hard taskmaster; when I was weak, he had total control over me.

FAMILY ROOTS

My father told me that his family believed that this idol, Vea, was a god. The spirits behind the idol seemed to help them solve their problems. They believed that it protected them every day. Therefore, when they began to travel to Ghana, they carried the idol, Vea, with them. In fact, the spirit behind the idol held them in bondage. The spirit, Vea, wanted to be carried on a human head. Once the trip began, it was forbidden that the idol could be removed from a man's head until they reached their destination. A man followed behind the one that was carrying the idol. During the trip, when the carrier got weak, the idol was moved from his head to the other man's head. Even while they were sleeping, the man whose head held the idol was required to lean against a tree. Throughout the night, the men of the tribe would take turns to change over. The family pressed onward. They walked through miles and miles those days through clouds of oppressive mosquitoes and ambushes in water filled with painful bloodsucking leeches. They stopped only for brief rest periods. They continued on the hard journey. So, the demons led them to carry the idol from Upper Volta through the waters of Ghana in this manner.

So, when they got to Ghana, they decided to settle. The climate in Ghana was not as good as in Upper Volta. The sun was warmer, and the mosquitoes thicker at night. But such discomforts didn't stop my grandfather from building a thatched hut on a parcel at the far edge of the new village. My grandfather put the idol Vea down and called the village. Let me tell you, if a town, a village, a country is named after an idol, the spirit that is connected to that particular idol will bring every person in the area under its power! You see, as far as the spirit is concerned, everyone is spiritually subjected to its power and under its domain. In such a way, that spirit will rule each person, unless spiritual eyes are opened by God to change the name of the area.

After my tribe settled down in Ghana, my grandfather became the head witch doctor and controlled the entire village through witchcraft. Because of this, the idol Vea was so powerful that many people were coming to my grandfather and my father for help. We became the established witch doctors' family in the area. Witch doctors are considered the most important people in the village—they rule.

THE BIRTH OF AN HEIR

After I was born, my father held a great celebration in honor of his firstborn son. All the elders of the village came together. My grandmother and the women prepared a sizeable feast. It was a great day for my father, because a baby boy had survived. They believed that this event showed great favor from the gods. Soon after my birth, I endured a cold bath to make me rugged. Then my body was rubbed with salt and red peppers. My screaming, struggling body, eyes full of tears, could not stop the ritualism that my father's tribe demanded.

Several days later, my mother prepared rice, leaves, corn, palm butter, and chunks of meat that were crammed down my throat. I was rubbed with sand and coconut bark to make me tougher. At the same time, this ritual was supposed to make me stronger. I was never allowed to have any other kind of milk apart from my mother's milk This was the beginning of my spiritual trek as the firstborn son.

CHOSEN BY THE SPIRIT GODS

My mother Mary was a docile, typical African woman. Her entire life was centered on her family. She had soft eyes. Although she had a tremendous impact on the formation of my life, my father had more sway. I was his first son and therefore, selected by the spirits to inherit the mantle of his supernatural power. I was dedicated to the devils before I was born. I remember my Mama told me that she felt the demons enter into her womb and heard the devils say, "He is our son."

DEMONIC ASSOCIATIONS

At a very young age, I knew by name many spirits that had power over of my mother and father. Although I was possessed in the womb of my mother, spirits came to me throughout my life.

My mother had considerable influence on my life and I was a delight to her. She had knowledge of the use of roots, herbs and other resources of witchcraft. Furthermore, she loved to study nature and had such passion for the animals of Africa. She taught me about the zebras, lions and giraffes.

"They make their homes, roaming across the wide, grassy plains," she said. "They are also the home of Africa's great elephants and monkeys. The leopards silently hunt for food in the rain forest. Then, camels live in the desert and they can go without water for a long time," she stated.

I remember being with my mother by the river watching the African birds that were so colorful. I saw the beautiful peacocks and flamingos. They are water birds that live in east and South Africa. The hyena lives in west and east Africa. Then there are the hippos. I loved the big lumbering hippos. There are two kinds in Africa and one weighs about eight thousand pounds. It is found all over Africa. The other is much smaller and is found only in Liberia and weighs about five hundred pounds.

My father owned a zoo of elephants, tigers and other animals. His father gave these animals to him. Before my father died, he gave them to me. I still have these animals and love to play with them. My lion is so tamed that he will bring my Bible to me. Well that is enough of the reminiscing about the animals.

Many times I saw my mother cry. She was sad, but whenever I questioned her, she tried to hide her tears.

"We had better go home, your father is waiting." She brushed her wet cheeks with her fingertips. Her gentle eyes twinkled as we started back to our village. Seldom did I ever see her smile.

FOLLOW THE FATHER

My father was a towering seven feet tall. He had to stoop under every doorway to enter into homes. Buildings shook violently when he entered, so he was one of the most intimidating and dominating figures in the city. Every time they saw him, many people shrank back in terror. He had sharp, penetrating tiger-like eyes that compelled attention. How majestic he was in stature. It was said that thousands of demons worshiped him.

In Africa, witch doctors hold a supernatural rule over the village chiefs. They sit on supernatural thrones. The chiefs know that they remain in power because of the mystical power of the witch doctors. Furthermore, chiefs and kings are often considered to be gods!

When you see my father and then see me, it's as if looking at his twin. Today it's amazing but when I look at his picture, it's like looking into a mirror except he is four inches taller. I am six-foot-six inches tall. My father held the respect of highest society. Everyone knew that he reigned with famed power and might because of his fearful, supernatural power. As a result of this power, he could look at a person and by his will that person would drop dead on the spot! Since I was raised in an idolatrous home, I didn't know that there was anything wrong with killing people until I received Jesus Christ. I had a demonic heart. Actually, I remember that I enjoyed seeing animals and people hurt or tortured.

Since early boyhood, I was chosen for a handpicked spiritual quest. The spirit world was more real to me than the natural world. I was about eight or nine years old when the demons first manifested themselves to me. In fact, they appeared as my friends. On many occasions, they manifested in the forms of people. Some were dressed in white robes while others took on the dress of local attire. They had both African and Indian names and these spirits became my closest friends. They took care of me and brought me toys and favorite foods to eat. At all times, I saw otherworldly warriors with African masks and spears surrounding me. My father told me that these were my ancestral spirits and their job was to watch over me. They were my guardian spirits. At a very early age, they taught me how to read people's minds and their palms. As I grew older, they brought ancient writings and taught me the bewitching meanings that were written in these witchcraft books. They helped me with everything, including hunting and schoolwork. They also taught me about the various idols that were worshiped in the village. One thing, they wanted to do was to keep me isolated from other people. It was important to keep me from anything normal and away from the things that the other children did. They told me that they liked me and would, at times, ask me if I liked them. Their presence seemed natural to me and seemed closer than my family members. Twenty-five thousand demons were controlling me.

DEMONIC FORMS

Demon entities use many different forms of control of humans, including having control over all the five senses. The manifestations are usually to announce their presence or to annoy humans. I could see their visual expressions as shadowy figures of human-like beings, animals, or strange objects, such as blocks that were used to block in people so that they could not accomplish things that they were trying to accomplish.

The appearances of these demons are related to the traditional signs of haunted places. Sometimes religious symbols, such as crucifixes and witchcraft emblems, such as hexagrams, pentagrams, six-six-six numbers, will appear on the walls. They take on different shapes and forms.

Demons range in size. Some can only be seen through powerful microscopes, appearing like microscopic germs, while others are as large as skyscrapers. Some appear as human figures such as men, women, and children. Others materialize as animals, insects, serpents, flies and mythical beings. Some are shadows that have animated creatures like shapes with membranous wings waffling just above their shoulders. Although they had arms and legs, they seemed to move about without using them. Some appeared as prehistoric lizards with scaly heads. I've also seen gargoyles with two huge yellow cat-eyes. They dart to and fro. Their bodies looked half humanoid, and half animalistic. Some were horrific, reptilian, and warty in appearance. Their demonic images can be seen on many computer games and rock music that are being sold worldwide.

These various demons have different functions. The spirit of witchcraft often appears as a half man-half goat. The upper half of the demonic body appears as a man. His face has the characteristic of a man with combined features of a goat, and from the waist down a goat with hooves. Often he wears nothing but sometimes he wears a vest and eyeglasses. In literature, the Hebrew refers to him as Satyr (Sater means Satan). The Greeks call him Pan or Faun. He rules over a group of demons that motivate occult activities that are related to witchcraft. He is also involved in sexual perversions.

These demons also travel down the family lines to enforce family curses upon their victims. Demons can give off strange putrid odors. Vivid ways to describe the odors are ghastly, musty, and they are sickening. These demonic odors permeate the air and remind me of "the smell of death." Earth-bound spirits go everywhere that humans do. They are constantly looking for ways to enter human beings' bodies. However, if they are not able to get the advantage to enter a person, they will enter an animal or an object. If they are living in an object, they will draw people to worship them.

Just as the devil can possess a person, he can and will posses an object or a house. This is the reason Israel was commanded by God to totally destroy the cities of Canaan. They had been involved in demonic activity and through their idol worship had become accursed places (Joshua 6:17,18). Demonically controlled places can be handled in two ways: destroy the place or deliver the place by prayer and dedicate the place to the worship of God (Joshua 6:24).

DEMONIC RELATIONSHIPS

I had lived with the demons ever since I can remember. Some were my friends while others were my enemies. Demons never talked in terms of love. I personally did not think in those terms. I had a demonized heart, hard and very cold. The demons would torture and hurt me if I failed to obey them. Sometimes I would fear them while other times I felt safe with them. Many times, I experienced seeing demons leaving bruises cuts and bites inflicted on human bodies. I saw them throwing objects used to block the blessings of the "rebellious people" (Satan called Christians "rebellion people"). Demons enjoy opening and closing doors and windows, hurling of books and stones, setting fires, projecting through the air many other things. Often, I've witnessed them killing people and throwing human beings around. This is their mission, to kill, rob and destroy.

The demons filled my dreams with their presence. They usually took me into other worlds and ethereally showed me things that are indescribable.

Yes, the demons are undeniable. But now, I've come to know the reality of Jesus. However, the church needs to be aware not only of the demonic power that is motivating the physical world, but also the sovereign power of Jesus Christ that is over them. I believe that behind every activity in the world that is not of God is demonic. I can point to the invisible spirit that hides the demonic power. The Antichrist Spirit is motivating this evil power.

Anytime we sample the fashions of the world, and we come in contact with the demonic power behind it. We must be very careful when we fellowship with unbelievers in the world. Remember that the activities of the spirit of the world do not honor or promote God's kingdom. The truth of this statement can be seen in the industries of entertainment, banking, military, medicine, law, commerce, sports, business, and even in some counterfeit Christian churches.

Many people in the entertainment industry will push sex, violence, witchcraft and rebellion, etc. Then too, many counterfeit Christian churches advance a form of a false religion without Jesus Christ at the center of its activities. Jesus will remove His candlestick from any church that will not teach His Word and will not keep Him as preeminent in its life. They will lose His protection.

Chapter Three

The Bushman

There shall not be found among you anyone that maketh his son or his daughter to pass through the fire, or that useth divination, or an observer of times, or an enchanter, or a witch, Or a charmer, or a consulter with familiar spirits, or a wizard, or a necromancer. For all that do these things is an abomination unto the Lord: and because of these abominations the Lord thy God doth drive them out from before thee. (Deuteronomy 18:10–12)

TRIBAL INITIATION

I was a young boy and the drums were beating furiously. The moon was full and the night animals were making their sounds. The village men lit their torches and were drinking potions. I had witnessed many tribal rituals; however, tonight it was different because I was the one who was going to be initiated. My mouth became dry as a cottonmouth snake. A shower of fear flooded every nerve cell of my body. I stood bravely by my father with my teeth clinched tightly together. I was being very careful not to show the explosions of panic inside. My father, Aloriga, had his arm around my shoulder. His eyes were like steel. Yet, I could see the pride that mapped his face.

Abruptly a short, stocky figure materialized, clothed in animal hides and furry pelts. He made a hand leap over a mound. Then, he held his head back and began to take deep breaths as though sniffing something in the air. I recognized the costume was the ancestral raiment of my father's Frafra tribal shaman. His face was totally hidden behind a painted bright yellow, blue green carved African mask. As he twisted around, I could see his circled eyes, ruby-red mouth, and four multicolored strips on his cheeks. He had an elongated staff with tiny pieces of feathers attached by colorful strings, dangling stones and dried grasses.

African drums, music and dance were working together to celebrate our African traditions. Nevertheless, the tribal masks that were worn during harvest celebrations and rites of passage were intimidating to me. These masks are also used during dances for the birth of new babies, weddings and funerals. These gruesome masks are conjured up by the witch doctors into hideous representations of demon gods. Really, the witch doctors are reproducing images that they have seen in their contact with evil spirits.

The other men were wearing antelope horns, animal teeth, gourds, knives, iron bracelets and leather pouches. Both sexes in Africa are often mutilated on the face or body as part of this all-pervasive charm cult. Mutilations, bizarre to western eyes, take the form of scars, filing down of teeth, extending the lips or ears with discs or rings, and plugging the nostrils.

I watched as the drumbeat, chants and the waves of hands ensued. The African shaman slithered like a snake, then explosively forward while drums boomed a jungle beat with the rhythm of his feet. Gyrating to the sounds with the grace of a cat, he circled, examining me with black menacing eyes, the mask moving with his dance. He sang invoking the power of the gods. I had witnessed many animal and human sacrifices before this time but was now this was a personal experience. Even so, my father had spiritually prepared me for this moment. Smiling, he stood proudly, with his arms around my shoulders. He knew that this was the beginning of my long spiritual journey into his world of witchcraft and supernatural power. As the witch doctor cavorted and chanted around the fire, I stood still, frozen with fear but I dared not show it. I bit my upper lip as blood slid through my veins like needles when a goat was sacrificed. Its blood splattered everywhere.

The knife still glistened with red drops of blood from the mutilated goat as I rubbed my tongue against the back of my mouth. Then, I was told to dip my finger into the blood and repeated the oath of the rites of passage. As he conjured his magic, the witch doctor danced, clapped and chanted some more. Then he invited the gods to join him.

He rubbed ritual oils and the goat's blood on my face. There were thousands of spirits cheering and watching when he took a sharp knife and slashed my cheeks with deep gashes. I flinched for a second with the pain but I dared not show any reaction. I felt my warm blood running down my face. He thrust his finger into his witches' box and traced the freshly cut wound with a magical black powder. This was done to fortify and spiritually strengthen me. Then, I was given a staff with an emblem of my future spiritual authority and my grandfather's mask. Additionally, there was a large kettle boiling, filled with mystical portions and human flesh. A bloodthirsty demon was stalking the sacrifice. With that, I was commanded by the witch doctor to drink and eat. The human flesh and blood felt warm going down my throat. My blood was still flowing down my cheeks. Then the witch doctor packed up his gear and went off into the bush. It was quite an impressive ceremony for a young boy of twelve.

It took longer than usual for my gashes to heal because the scars did not heal well. They became infected and inflamed and drew armies of flies to attack the wound. This caused the scars to become broader on my cheeks. Today, they remain dark scars across my cheeks. I remember walking around the village, wearing the marks as a symbol of superiority. Everyone in the tribe encouraged me because of my birthright and my future status of power.

Today the tribal black scars are still deeply etched upon my face. Thank God that Jesus can erase the spiritual significance of the marks in the spirit realms. The Holy Spirit has put a new mark on my face. He supernaturally placed his seal upon my forehead and I am now marked for heaven.

Then He told me that visible scars on my face, only serve to show the world of the testimony of my past. I thank Jesus that my sons do not have these demonic scars on their faces. It really happened, and the powers of those rituals are now blotted out forever. My name is blotted out of Satan's Book of Death and my name is listed in the Lamb's Book of Life, praises to His Holy Name forevermore.

INVESTIGATION OF THE BUSH

My father, Aloriga, was about to give his powers over to me. Normally, in Africa, we give everything we have to our next of kin, our firstborn son. The boy, even if he is the third child, is supposed to take over the father's place. My father wanted to relinquish his powers to me because he was about sixty or sixty-five. At that time, he believed that he was going to die soon. He wanted to teach me certain things about his supernatural powers.

My father was training me to take his spiritual mantle. He told me the introduction to the spirits from the sky and the land (bush) was very important to my future.

These demons in the forest are called dwarfs. There are also the marine demons of the sea.

"In the beginning." he said, "when the demons fell from the skies, they fell in the bushes, the mountains, the seas and some fly in the skies." (You can see these spiritual kingdoms described in the Bible, in Job 38:31, 33; Job 41:22; Job 9:9; Isaiah 23:11).

When my father told me about these demons, I was thunder struck and I didn't know what to say. So I said nothing.

The night that we made a trip into the bush, it was about midnight. I learned that the powers of darkness always work in the night. We walked about three kilometers through the brush and bramble, deep into the forest. At the brow of the hill we stopped and gazed across the green jungles of the northeast. It was a wild rough land. Roving herds of wild elephants, pythons and strange tribesmen hardly known to the outside world populated it. Father told me that I had to learn about all the demons of the bush.

"We had to have contact with those demons too," he assured me.

"They are very powerful."

I clearly remember that night, when the moon hung in the sky like a giant opal casting light and shadows as we walked through the brush. A majestic elephant stood under the shadows of the trees. With his trunk proudly raised. This noble creature had caught my undivided attention for a moment. The elephant has long been the symbol of status and power.

Suddenly my eyes caught a spiritual being that was shaped like a winged stallion flying across the sky.

"Oh!" I said, pointing excitedly. "Look at that wonderful horse!"

"That is Pegasus, son. He is a white winged horse that performs many amazing feats. He is the son of the god, Zeus. It is a rare thing to see this spiritual horse. It is a sign of your great future."

Soon we came to the bush. In this part of the forest, I saw some of the most bizarre looking demons. At first, I was startled at the grotesque appearance of these demons. As a matter of fact, in the beginning I really did not want to have anything to do with them. Except that my father told me, "Take care of the gods and they will take care you."

I was truly struck with terror when I met all the bush spirits. They made quite an astonishing impression on me. These dwarfed spirits were really scary. They were in the form of dwarfs, monstrous looking creatures. They stood bent over, hunchbacks with gnarled heads that protruded from scrunched shoulders. Some had flaming swords and warrior guardians of the high places. They looked strong, like brutal savages that visited people in nightmares. Intimidated, I held my father's hand tightly. The hair stood up at the nape of my neck as stark fear was sweeping over my body. Yet, they grinned at me through their large leathery jowls and jagged teeth. They didn't speak and didn't move but with bulged eyes, they watched me with their cold, piecing gazes.

My father taught me their secret ceremonies. I had to study their languages so that I could talk to the gods in their own languages and tongues. I had to learn the various gods' favorite foods and preferred drinks. For instance, one god could desire a rooster or goat for dinner and his favorite drink alcohol, while another demon god could desire human flesh and blood.

My father warned me, "Son, don't be afraid. You have to go and make a covenant with them. You see, whenever they strike a person and if that person comes to you for help, you will have the power to help them. It's important, you will have to pacify these spirits so that you can work your supernatural powers for the people." He revealed to me that these spirits were not dependable.

He went on to say, "Then the spirits will give that person a release for a year or two, then suddenly, they will strike that person again. These spirits do not like people."

I discovered that demons are no man's friends. In practice, they really want to destroy all people. My father pointed out that there were many people who were targeted by these spirits for death. They use the witch doctors to conjure up incantations, potions and blood sacrifices to kill their enemies.

My father said, "A witch or wizard has to be very careful when they throw a curse, and under what terms."

He told me that knowledgeable witch doctors would always "examine with caution" or scan (called remote viewing) the person before sending a curse.

He said, "If the magic power of the intended victim is stronger than the witch or wizard of the curse believed it to be, or if the curse is not correctly cast, the curse will bounce back upon the person who threw it in the first place."

STRANGE RITUALS

One night we walked into the jungle. A ghostly mist hung among the trees. The gray moon darted between the hills. We could hardly see where we walked. My father seemed to know the area like the back of his hand. Strange feelings rested inside, and my heart was strongly pumping. Suddenly we came to a bizarre clearing. The sounds of chanting native witch doctors filled the air.

I saw dog heads that were dangling from a nearby cave entrance. There were piles of bloodied skinned animals with their hearts cut out that were being prepared to burn in a raging fire. The priests were in a frenzy. The ritual had begun when all of a sudden a bull was killed. The witch doctor slit its throat. Another man placed a large bowl under its neck to catch the bull's blood. Everyone bowed to the god of Baal to honor his blood for the ritualism. They seemed to enjoy these morbid fantasies and animal tortures.

Large amounts of rice and red peppers were prepared for a feast. Some men were sitting on blocks of wood or stones. Some were squatting. Everyone used their fingers to eat because there were no utensils. Each had a small clay bowl of rice. Then my father took a gourd jug and poured water on my head. My heart was pounding. After everyone had eaten their fill, naked men were dancing and chanting in the high places.

High places are where people sacrifice to the god of the area and so become dwelling place of demonic spirits. God commands the children of Israel to "demolish all their high places," (Numbers 33:52).

The demons watched and suddenly a shrill whistle pierced the air. A wave of terror raced throughout my body. Struggling for control, all of a sudden, I saw my father's face twist and become gnarly. Actually, he was being possessed by a god-spirit. When the spirit entered his body, father began to moan and shriek. Stark fear filled my mind when I saw him violently shake and writhe on the ground. Then his eyes became highly glazed. On the spur of the moment, he appeared to have an epileptic fit. All at once, he became entranced, passed out and fell to the ground. The demons were howling, hooting and laughing with glee. Abruptly, I felt my insides moving and tightening with terror but struggled to show no emotion. It was a hellish ordeal. A voice in my head said, "be calm, you are learning."

The dwarfs began to sing and dance near the fire. There was such a demonic gleam reflected in their faces. Watching from the bush, there were nebulous shadows lurking nearby. All at once, I heard a piercing scream that broke through the clouds of smoke. Goose bumps raced down my spine as I became very alert as the stench of burning flesh filled the night. Soon, the body of a young boy was cooked. The demons were in frenzy. My heart was beating furiously with fear. I hoped that soon it would be over. My young heart had not yet been demonized to a sufficient degree to see these evil matters.

ANCIENT DEMON GODS

Later, my father taught me about the ancient demon gods. "These gods are worshiped by their priests that burn incense in the high places to the idol gods of the mountains of Ghana. They burn incense to Baal, the sun, the moon and the planets to the hosts of heaven," he explained.

As a Christian, now, I know that God calls them hosts of heaven gods. "Lest thou lift up thine eyes unto heaven, and when thou seest the sun, and the moon, and the stars, (even) all the host of heaven, shoulders be driven to worship them, and serve them, which the Lord thy God hath divided unto all nations under the whole heaven" (Deuteronomy 4:19).

Thank God that the glorious Gospel that transforms from darkness to light and from death to resurrection, saved me. In fact the Gospel lives in the Book of Galatians. The golden text of Paul's letter to the Galatians is found in these words, "I am crucified with Christ: nevertheless I live; yet not I, but Christ liveth in me: and the life which I now live in the flesh I live by the faith of the Son of God, who loved me, and gave himself for me" (Galatians 2:20). This of its own supernatural power is the one and only plan that God has ordained to save sinners. I was a sinner. I am saved by His wonderful grace.

Chapter Four

Demonic Anointing

Wherefore, my dearly beloved, flee from idolatry. (1 Corinthians 10:14)

INHERITED CURSES

I remember when my father told me the story of how he received the demonic powers from his father. The family members were doing their rituals pouring out libations that make the dead body possess a demonic presence as it is laid in state. The rings and handkerchiefs that are given to the dead symbolize a covenant with the dead. When my grandfather died, the family had gathered for the funeral. The women were preparing food for the funeral, such as rice water, koko, tea and soups. Family heads are aware of this ritual of preparing special waters named "Adukrom Nsu." This is a concoction of ingredients so filthy, but added to the tea Koko, tea, soups and others for consumption. It is demonic. The family puts on black garments for three to six months when bereaved. This invites the spirits of death to stay in the house for a long time. Of course, borrowed clothes for funerals will act as a method to transfer spirits.

The mourners were chanting for the gods to descend and possess the worshipers in which the ancestral spirits were invoked to give oracles and be a power in the household. My father told me, "my grandfather was lying in the black coffin and his eyes snapped opened. His eyes looked like slits similar to a python snake. They were sunken into his head." Really it's a ghoulish idea.

As father described, the mourners were screaming and wailing and pleading that the spirit of the deceased will enter safely into the spiritual world. The black magicians and witch doctors were working their rituals.

Then all of a sudden, my grandfather was slowly getting into a sitting position. He swung his feet to the floor. He was in a total trance-like state with bulging-glazed eyes. His arms were still waving as he stood up. Trembling, he began a staggering and stumbling manner of walking. Furthermore, the demons made his body walk around the room.

Everyone in the room began weeping, wailing and screaming in loud voices. Something supernatural was happening. Something is happening, very scary. Yet to his loved ones, it was eerie but they thought it was quite wonderful. Awkwardly, moving unsteadily and lumbering across the room, the powers of darkness were in complete control of his body.

"That's the spirit of Voodoo," someone yelled.

"Yes, it's the god of the graveyard, Baron Samedi!" another exclaimed. "He's the devouring and lustful voodoo king of the cemetery spirits—spirit of death, and one of the more powerful spirits of the voodoo pantheon."

At this time, my grandfather told my father that he wanted to pass his powers to him before he could pass onto the other world. He asked my father to bring three bowls to him. Then my grandfather vomited, filling the bowls. He commanded my father to drink it. My father obeyed. Then after my father drank it my grandfather lay back in the casket and father was empowered with his spirits. Grandfather's mantle had passed to my father.

VOODOO POWERS

The word voodoo comes from the word Vodun, (meaning god, spirit, or sacred object) in the Fon language of West Africa. Voodoo is a system focusing on a distant god known as the Grand Master, who manifests through various rituals. He has a pantheon of demons, such as benevolent ones invoked by nada rites and harsher demons invoked by bloody petro rites. It consists primarily of the worship of ancestors and a hierarchy of gods. These demons seek to manifest themselves by taking "possession" of their worshipers during their frenzied dances. These ancestral spirit deities are known collectively as Loa. A major voodoo philosophy is, "Take care of the gods and they will take care of you."

Accordingly, during the voodoo ceremonies, the "Chief Bab" (short for babalawo, or priest) drinks human blood and chants, and dances savagely, which may continue for days on end. The initiate collapses and will fall into trances. Then possession takes place by these demons. In this altered state of consciences, the possessing demon may manifest itself and begin to speak, sing or curse as well as offer advice or cure the sick. Whenever the demon that has descended and entered their bodies possessed by voodoo worshipers, they usually shriek or howl. Some violently shake or writhe, as if experiencing an epileptic fit. On the spur of the moment, the possessed person will become entranced. He will pass out and fall to the ground. While in the trance, by the power of demons, some worshipers walk over broken glass or burning coals. Others place their hands in burning oil or alcohol. Voodoo advocates vow that if worshipers show no bodily harm after such practices, it means that demons have entered into their bodies.

In Africa, witch doctors really can create zombies who are also known as the "living dead." They are not fictional! The dead body has a blank glassy stare, a plastic face, filled with terror, and slow lumbering movement like a puppet. The voodoo belief is that a spirit can then be made to obey, mechanically, the wishes of the voodoo priest. He can, through demonic possession, reanimate a corpse. People are very scared of voodoo power.

Some of the voodoo symbols are such things as fetishes, icons, and voodoo dolls. Other symbols are to protect the wearer against poisoning, death hexes, evil spirits, sickness, injury and accidents. Voodoo is an occult religion rooted in Satanism. Tempting possession is also tempting serious spiritual risk.

My father taught me how to prepare the food for the living dead.

"Vagalas, you must not eat the food yourself," father advised. "Remember that your grandfather died during the last moon. He watches me every minute and I will never forget him. He will eat this food."

"So you think my grandfather is one of the living dead?" I asked my father as I stirred the yams and eggs together.

"Yes," father answered firmly. "He may be invisible to you, but that doesn't mean that he and other ancestors aren't watching over what we do. Your grandfather will be watching over you too. He tells me that you are his pride and joy."

When he finished building his altar, he filled his bowl with rice, beans, seeds, a lizard and three snails. He was satisfied with his task. He sat under the shade of a mango tree and watched me finish filling my bowl.

TRAINING WITH FATHER

My father told me, "Son, you want to be powerful in the spiritual realms, so you will have to know these demons from the bush, sky and the sea."

We started. We met those demons that are in charge of marriages. If a Christian is married and the Church has not blessed that marriage, the demons have an open door. If a Christian goes to the witch doctor for help, the door is open for demonic control. The demons can manipulate, intimidate, suppress, oppress and destroy. Then there are demons in charge of cancer, and diabetes. I learned how to work with these powers of evil.

However, during this time, I didn't know that a day was coming that I would stand in front of the people of God to expose these demons. I just thought that I was learning to become very powerful like my father. When the Lord called me to reveal the reality of these evil powers to His church, Jesus told me, "Many demons have my church and My people blinded. I am anointing you to expose the demons and you must tell My church how to defeat these demons and protect themselves."

Chapter Five

The City Under the Sea

Therefore rejoice, ye heavens, and ye that dwell in them. Woe to the inhabitants of the earth and of the sea! For the devil is come down unto you, having great wrath, because he knoweth that he hath but a short time. (Revelation 12:12).

INTRODUCTION TO SEA SPIRITS

I know that many will not believe this testimony concerning the City Under the Sea. They, in fact, will want to believe that it is just a fairy tale. They will try comparing it to something like the stories of "The Little Mermaid" or "The Wizard of Oz." Believe me. The city under the sea does spiritually exist. I know, because I personally spent twelve years under the sea and knew that it's a real place. This is my testimony of residing with the demon gods under the sea. Powerful testimony!

MY SPIRITUAL TRANSFORMATION

Finally the time came that my father took me to the sea where he got most of his power. This was a gate to a city under the sea where people get gifts for wizardry.

Seagulls were swirling across the gentle waves. The setting sun was a hazy circle behind the gray clouds dipping beyond the horizon. The skyline was marked by the shading between the gray-blue of the sea and the blue-gray of the sky. Suddenly the sun sank out of sight. The moonlit night darkened, I felt the restless splendor of the sea.

I sensed hundreds of eyes that may or may not be human silently watching from the waves.

Finding a rock half in and half out of the water, we climbed upon it to rest. For a moment, I watched the little creatures of the deep as they leaped free of the pull of the tide. Then, in the distance, I saw a form that rose from the crest of the waves. Sea foam crowning his green-dark hair, his hands were raised above his head. He seemed to stand for a moment on his tail. In one instant, with a great splash, he disappeared into the depths of the sea.

"Wow! Did you see him father?"

"Yes, Vagalas," replied my father. "He's called a merfolk and there are mermaids too. They are scattered throughout seas around the world. Most people who have seen them believe that they are just imaginations, but they are actually spirits in one of their many forms. This is the beginning of a great adventure. Here you will meet the "spirits of the sea."

Then my father gave me one of his powerful potions. His eyes were glazed, shimmered like small sea lights, then turned glassy as the potions began to take effect. I began to feel airy. This form of entrance into a fantasy world is enhanced through drugs or potions, especially the hallucinogenic kind.

These drugs are so effective in transporting a person through the spirit world that they are highly sought after by witches and wizards worldwide. On the spur of the moment, my father blasted forth with a strong whistle sound and instantly two very powerful demons appeared. All of a sudden, I felt my spirit releasing itself out of my body. One of the demons entered into it and took control to keep my body alive while my spirit was not there. I felt as free as a bird. My father's spiritual body was moving to take my hand. I turned my head back to see on the rock sitting our bodies as we started walking toward the sea. Our bodies appeared to be alive! It was eye deceiving, as the bodies were moving and gesturing to each other against the dusk of the night.

Although the night air was still, the endless tidal waves crashed against the shoreline. When we came to the edge of the sea, my father simply tapped the sea with his foot. To my utter amazement, instantly the sea divided into a dry pathway. I could see the fishes and sea creatures on both sides of the raised water. They were swimming and churning by the sides of the raised water. It looked like mirrored walls as we entered the water. It was a strange sight. He took me by the hand and we began walking down into the ropes of mist into the sea. It was very supernatural, yet to me it felt natural. The Bible includes a nether world in these prophetical words: "There also God highly exalted him (Christ) and bestowed on Him the name which is above every name that at the name of Jesus every knee should bow, of those who are in heaven, and on earth, and under the earth…" (Philippians 2: 9–10). And the Word of God speaks of the sea as a place that gives "up the dead which were in it" (Revelation 20:13).

Little did I know at this time that I was beginning to go through a great spiritual shift that was going to bring about the capture of my soul by Satan. I was entering the hadean world of Satan and his demons. These are mysterious experiences that very few ever return to talk about. The cresting currents continued to move apart as we walked descending down to the bottommost part of the sea. I stopped and picked up one of the beautiful shells. Putting the shell against my ear, I could hear the beating heart of the sea. All at once, there were flickering lights and moving shadows. They darted behind a roughened mountainous hill that was covered with seaweed. A group of large living things was swirling around. These beings were somewhat larger than men. Their flippers could never be mistaken for arms.

"Are they sea monsters?" I asked.

"No son," he answered, "just a group of playful whales."

I turned to look back to see the water roaring and crashing together. The sea seemed to be taking it last breath of fresh air as it thundered shut behind us. I saw a pale white light unsteadily shining. I felt the dry sand sticking under my feet. My father held my hand tightly.

"We are almost there." He had a devilish look on his face. A gnarly dark figure sat upon a coral bed. He did not look at us or make a move as we passed by.

CASTLES UNDER THE SEA

My father and I began descending deeper into sea on dry ground. Soon stepped onto a broad highway that led to a brilliant light radi ated in the distance. "Look father," I exclaimed! "It shines and glitters like a jewel."

"Yes son. We are going to the great city under the sea," my father replied. "Not many people are ever able see it."

Many highways from various provinces of Ghana are joined to this big highway. A majestic city came into view that was located in the center of the sea! Soon we arrived at the brilliant city that seems to be without beginning or end as if it were made by magic. All at once, I found myself walking through the gates of the most mystical, delightful city on earth. It was beyond dreams and visions.

My father said, "This is where your training will begin, my son," He put his arm around m shoulder. "You will be strong and powerful because you were born for this position." According to my father this is a place where god put his power.

It is impossible for me to describe to you the splendor of this awesome place. Physically you won't see it but spiritually you can see it. However, I have never seen a city on this earth more beautiful than this mysterious underwater metropolis. There were giant futuristic crystal skyscrapers and brilliant lazar lights bedazzling the currents of the sea. It was a spellbinding place, beyond words, it reminds you of a spiritual Disney World. The streets were made of gold—not real gold but something that appeared like gold. There is nothing in the world that could compare to this enchanting place, such a stunning, majestic, and ravishing habitation. It was apocalyptical, fairyland.

HIDDEN CITY UNDER THE SEA

The city under the sea is not a hidden place from many people of Africa. In fact there are many spiritual cities that are located around the world. In every country in the world, you will find the same structures and human activities under the lakes and rivers which affects the lives of those on the earth above. Actually, there are highways under the sea that connect these spiritual cities! Since my salvation, the Lord Jesus has saved and delivered many African wizards and witches have testified about the existence of these spiritual cities that are located off the sea coasts around the world!

The mysterious city that I was assigned is a supernatural place that is located under the sea off the coast of Ghana and it extends to the Bermuda Triangle off the coast of Bermuda. The region located near the coast of Ghana is the area where hurricanes develop. Satan sends the wizards and witches to conjure these destructive disasters. These sorcerers release the gods of destruction. The city is made of the substance where imaginations fail, beyond human belief and is the most spectacular habitation in the world.

Notice that I quoted (Revelation 12:12) for you at the heading of this chapter. Observe that the Bible says, "woe to the inhabitants of the earth and the sea!" The Bible clearly says that there are inhibitors (spiritual beings) living in the lands and the sea. Yes, It is true. I know because I've lived and worked there for Satan's kingdom.

It is in these demonic cities that Satan trains his agents to steal the souls of men, women and children.

DWELLING PLACE FOR DEMONS

The city that I lived in for twelve years is located near the coast of Ghana. This city is highly organized. The sorcery world is real and highly organized. It is formed administratively and political structure that follows the same patterns as in our worldly governments. In the sorcery government women hold the highest positions. In fact, Satan is documenting everything about people on the earth. There is a "Book of the Dead" where every evil deed is recorded about people on the earth. These records are carefully kept so that the demons can legally enslave and control the people that are living around the globe. He will also use these records to testify against these people before the throne of God after the end of the world. He knows everything that is hidden away in people's secret lives. This is why the Antichrist is going to be able to rule the world when his time comes. He has no power unless people give it to him in their rebellion against God.

THE GATES OF POWER

The Bible reveals that the spirits dwelling under the sea do exist. But somehow Satan has been able to bewitch Christians from being able to see these Scriptures. When I got saved, Christian teachers were saying that the Antichrist comes out of the sea. Then they would say that the "word sea, represented the masses of people." They could not spiritually see these Scriptures through the eyes of the Holy Spirit.

For instance carefully look at the description of the imagery of the beast in the Bible. "And I stood upon the sand of the sea, and saw a beast rise up out of the sea, having seven heads and ten horns, and upon his horns ten crowns, and upon his heads the name of blasphemy" (Revelation 13:1).

According to many Bible commentators, this "beast" is the end-time Antichrist. The "beast" represents two things: 1. He is a demon prince who presently is locked up in the "abyss" and will be released in the end-time Tribulation. (Revelation 11:7). This is the same beast here that is coming up out of the sea from the "abyss." 2. This beast possesses a mortal man and this man receives power from the dragon (Satan) in the end time (Revelation 13:4–10). The demon prince that comes up out the abyss possesses this mortal man. (Revelation 11:7).

This sea city is very organized into levels of spiritual power. For instance, if a person goes to a soothsayer or a witch, that person legally gives Satan power over his soul. Then, the witch or soothsayer would have to give authority of the person's soul to Satan. Truthfully, even if a person is taken to one of these occultists as a child by a parent, then only a Christian who knows the superior power of Jesus Christ can break it. Their past must be destroyed. Whenever a demon is invited in, he must be kicked out!

This mysterious sea city is filled with surprises but it is also very scientific. For example, whenever I wanted a cup of coffee, I'd just press a button and it would appear immediately. Many inventions are devised here. I saw computers here before they ever appeared on the earth.

There are also well equipped research centers for sorcerers where their scientists, doctors, and mechanics work. Some of these people are working consciously and some do so consciously. Many things that we see in the world are manufactured by sorcery.

ABADDON, KING OF THE ABYSS

The Bible speaks of supernatural beings coming out of the sea in the Book of Revelation. "They have as king over them, the angel of the abyss; his name in Hebrew is Abaddon, and in the Greek he has the name Apollyon." (Revelation 9:11).

The supernatural beings, Leviathan and Rahab roam the seas and fight for the control of the entrance to Sheol-Hades. During the coming tribulation period, these evil forces will finally gain release of their comrades below, including their king—Abaddon. The Lord will allow Satan to release two demonic orders from Sheol Hades: One, The scorpion-centaurs, (Revelation 9:1–11). The two hundred million demon horsemen shown in (Revelation 9:13–21).

In both these groups we see the shapes of horses. These scorpion-centaurs, whose appearance is like a horse and scorpion, are turned lose during the tribulation to torment men for five months, (Revelation 9:5). Whatever this torment is, the Bible doesn't say, except the curse of this plague is that "men will seek death and will not find it. They will long to die and death flees from them" (Revelation 9:6).

In Revelation 9:1-11 will be the release of the depraved demons and fallen angels currently locked in the Abyss. The Bible teaches that the Abyss is a spirit prison (Luke 8:31; 1 Peter 3:19; 2 Peter 2:4; Jude 6).

In the Abyss, some of the fallen angels are now bound in "everlasting chains under darkness" waiting "for the judgment of the great day."

In Revelation 9:11, an intriguing character is introduced: They have as king over them, the angel of the Abyss; his name in Hebrew is Abaddon, and in the Greek he has the name Apollyon. (Nasu)

Abaddon and Apollyon both mean "destroyer." Who is this ruling demon called the "Destroyer," who is released from the Abyss during God's wrath on mankind in the last days of this age?

Chapter Six

Creatures Beneath the Sea

Such knowledge is too wonderful for me; it is high. I cannot attain unto it. Whither shall I go from thy spirit? or whither shall I flee from thy presence? If I ascend up into heaven, thou art there: if I make my bed in hell, behold, thou art there. If I take the wings of the morning, and dwell in the uttermost parts of the sea; Even there shall thy hand lead me, and thy right hand shall hold me. If I say, Surely the darkness shall cover me; even the night shall be light about me. Yea, the darkness hideth not from thee; but the night shineth as the day: the darkness and the light are both alike to thee. For thou hast possessed my reins: thou hast covered me in my mother's womb. (Psalms 139:6–13)

PICTURES UNDER THE SEA

I saw many handsome men and beautiful young girls. There were also young children there. I was introduced to them and warmly welcomed. The children play games with mermaids. Mermaids look like humans from the waist up, but fishes from the waist down. The boundary between the human area and fish area happens in the pelvis. This area is part human-like and fish-like (the outside of this area is fish). She is truly a beautiful appearing spirit. She is very popular with the children under the sea.

Disembodied demons lurked in the shadows of the room. Under helmets with drawn swords, stone-faced demons glared at the scene with their emotionless, cold eyes. The giant fallen angels of Genesis stood guarding the entrance to the city. The Ascended Masters (high-level ruling spirits) watched in glee. The smiles on their lips disguised the reality of the evil that was lurking in their hearts. The Bible shows that supernatural beings live in the sea. "And I stood upon the sand of the sea, and saw a beast rise up out of the sea, having seven heads and ten horns, and upon his horns ten crowns, and upon his heads the name of blasphemy. And the beast which I saw was like unto a leopard, and his feet were as the feet of a bear, and his mouth as the mouth of a lion: and the dragon gave him his power, and his seat, and great authority" (Revelation 13:1–2).

This exotic spiritual city under the sea is the place where I trained to become a wizard. Here, I learned to practice the deception for Satan and learn his strategies to help him win the world for his evil cause. He really believes that he will rule over the people in the world and they will worship him. His plans not only included deceiving people in the world but also consisted of bewitching the backslider people in the Christian churches.

The Bible says, "My people are destroyed for a lack of knowledge" (Hosea 4:6). Understand this, Satan knows that he is defeated, but he also recognizes Christians' lack of knowledge. I tell you, and he knows it. This is the reason why he can take the advantage of people. He works freely in many churches because only a few are able to discern his works and hardly anyone ever believes them.

The Bible unveils the reality that the sea does hold supernatural creatures. The leviathan is described as a frightening monster of the seas in Job 41. He is called Leviathan. His name occurs five times in the Old Testament, always as an evil entity allied with Satan. This spirit is called King of the sea!

Rahab is the name of another demonic inhabitant. Rahab is called a fleeing sea serpent in (Job 26:12,13). In Job 6, "Abyss Under the Sea" is likened to Egypt, whose army was drowned in the Red Sea. God's people were more powerful thereby overcoming and crushing the evil entity over those waters.

SPIRITUAL ACTIVITY—TRANSFORMING

When I was very young, Satan gave me the power to change into five different animals: a snake, crocodile, butterfly, lizard, and crab. This ability means that I was considered to be a middle-class wizard.

A demon told me that he had the power to affect transformations with humans. I asked, "What does that mean?"

"I can change humans to the forms of animals," the demon replied. "I can change humans into animals or vice versa!"

I laughed and suddenly, he changed me into a snake. I got so excited and wanted to leave the room and go and play in this new body. I looked at the door, but it was locked. I wanted to open it, but Satan told me to just think about it and it would happen. So I thought about going through the door and I did! Without realizing that I had the same mind, just a different body, my changed body began to slither on the ground like a snake. Then he changed me back. I asked him how that benefited his kingdom—or, did he do that just to show off his power? He got angry and challenged me to never underestimate his power again. He said, "You'd better never laugh at me again."

"It's all about power and rebellion," he said. All at once, he changed me into a butterfly and then a lizard. I was able to fly and go through walls with these new body forms and I was moved by my mind power. I became more and more intrigued with the powers of the demonic world.

BLACK MAGIC

These powers are being described in demonic books, cartoons and movies. The dictionary definition of a werewolf is "...a person transformed into a wolf or capable of assuming the form of a wolf." This transformation is not unique in Satanism, but it is done only at the highest levels of witchcraft. Severe demonic possession is also required. This spiritual process is also called "shape shifting," is done with the power of demons and they can assume other forms than just a wolf! If you have been paying attention, you have noticed several TV shows and movies that have depicted this power such as *Roswell, Wolf* with Jack Nicholson, *American Werewolf in London, American Werewolf in Paris, Buffy the Vampire Slayer, Teen Wolf* with Michael J. Fox and The Harry Potter books and movies. These supernatural powers are shown in these films.

"Necronomicon" has its place in modern black magic and "Transyuggothian" metaphysics. For example, there is now a whole line of materials based on the hellish, Lovecraft "Cthulhu mythos," a form of magic practiced in the darkest Satanism—a system of magic prominently featured in The Satanic Rituals! The Necronomicon and the Cthulhu mythos are quite real. "Lycanthropy" is the clinical term for being (or believing yourself to be) a werewolf. These are immensely complicated worlds of magic, spells and violence.

As a child, I was taught how to change a lizard into a crocodile or a frog to a fly. Flies were sent to put sickness or bad luck on people by biting them or stepping on their food and leaving behind poison or witchcraft. Other sorcerers change into flies to be carried on people's shoulders.

FANTASY WORLD

Fantasy is the world to which every wizard seeks constant access. It is a world filled with exciting adventures with magic awaiting them at every step. A wizard will consider his fantasy world to be more exciting, more fulfilling, than his real world.

Children are vulnerable to powerful images precisely because they are at a stage of development when their fundamental concepts of reality are being formed. Satan is having a field day with the kids, producing books of terror to putrefy and trash mind and soul. Children have always been highly susceptible to fantasies and fairy stories, to amazing flights of the imagination. Keep the children from reading feigned fables, vain fantasies and wanton stories. Fantasy and fable are now popular and widely received that even so-called Christian fiction fantasy novels for kids are in vogue. They slyly and cunningly move the young reader from Christianity into an imaginary realm of darkness. Many times, even mature adult Christians find difficulty in discerning the true nature of these books.*

You must protect your children. Satan is very busy capturing their hearts. Once they are entrapped, it is very difficult to reverse his spiritual damage to their lives.

Jesus Christ believed in, dealt with, and referred to the devil at least 15 times, and the Bible refers to him 114 times. The Lord was not talking about an imaged or mythological being, but a real supernatural being who is described by the Bible as the arch deceiver of

---

* Texe Marrs, *Ravaged by the New Age: Satan's Plan to Destroy our Kids* (Living Truth Publishers, 1989).

all mankind. The Scriptures warn us there is such a being as the devil and there are such entities as evils spirits which are set against God and His creation.

DEVILS

There are many references to devils in Africa but despite the name, they seem to be rather benign creatures. They are described as having one eye, one leg, one arm and one ear, but they can run very fast. They have the ability to disguise themselves as humans. They live in villages the same as humans do and partake in the same activities (i.e. farming, hunting, feasting). They seem to be viewed as more of a nuisance than a threat.

> Hausa (West Africa): This tribe attributes many problems (medical or not) to the intervention and/or possession of an evil spirit. In order to cause the evil to leave or at least lessen the effects, a person who is familiar with the spirit dances for it (the dance is specific to the type of spirit). During the dance, the cause and cure of the evil is brought to light. The cure usually requires an animal sacrifice, typically a bird of some sort, color, and gender (again, this is specific to the spirit). The following is a list of the most prevalent evil spirits and the effects that they have:
>
> Dakaki or Mai-ja-Chikki: this spirit is said to resemble a serpent. It causes evil eye, an affliction that may lead to stomach ulcers.
>
> Kuri, Yerro or Yandu: this spirit is said to be a black hyena spirit. It causes paralysis.
>
> Ba-Maguje: this spirit has no description. It causes alcoholism by making the victim increasing thirsty and eventually insensible.
>
> Mai-Gangaddi or Sarikin Barchi. this spirit has no description. It causes sleeping sickness.
>
> Bidda: this spirit has no description. It causes stiffness.
>
> Taiki: this spirit has no description. It causes swelling of the stomach
>
> Rako: this spirit has no description. It causes weakness

and doziness in the old.

Kworrom: this spirit resides under tree roots. It causes travelers to trip and stumble.

Sarikin Bakka: this spirit is described as a nature spirit ruling over animals. It causes madness.

Jigo or Jihu: this spirit has no description. It causes fever, prickly heat and shivering.

Mahalbiya: this is a female spirit. She causes sores and tropical ulcers

Jato or Jakada or Janziri: this spirit is described as a "dirty" spirit, residing in sewers and gutters. It causes venereal disease which can lead to insanity.

Ba-Toye: this spirit is a fire spirit. It is related to burning houses, fields and trees.

Makeri (blacksmith) and Masaki (weaver): these spirits have no descriptions. They cause back, arm and work related illness in craftspeople.

Kishi: Kimbundu, Angola. The kishi is a man-eating demon who can disguise himself as a regular man so he can take a wife.

One tale of a kishi begins with the sea god Kianda and two sisters. Kianda wanted to find a wife and came across two sisters not far from the shoreline. He disguised himself as a skull and approached the sisters. He proposed to the first sister. She not only refused but hit him with a stick. Kianda then proposed to the second sister. She accepted his proposal and offered him food. Kianda asked her to follow him, which she did, to the sea. He flew towards a rock wall which opened when he approached. They entered and were immediately sealed inside. The young bride was then surrounded by servants who addressed her as their queen and dressed her in fine garments. Kianda shed his skull disguise and appeared before her in all his splendor. It was then she recognized him as Kianda the Sea God. From then on, they lived happily ever after and have many children. The children have human figures but can live underwater like fishes.

The tale continues with the story of the first sister. She

meets and marries a handsome young man. He takes her to his house, far from her village. To her horror, their first child is born with two heads—one human and one hyena. She realizes that her husband is a kishi, a demon who eats humans. Although she attempts to escape, the demon is much faster and captures her. He then devours her and her child is raised eating human flesh. †

† Heather Changeri, "African Demons," *WhiteRose's Garden, http://www.whiterosesgarden.com/Nature_of_Evil/Demons/DM_world_myths/african_demons.htm.*

Chapter Seven

Underwater Witchcraft

Therefore rejoice, ye heavens, and ye that dwell in them. Woe to the inhabiters of the earth and of the sea! for the devil is come down unto you, having great wrath, because he knoweth that he hath but a short time. (Revelation 12:12)

WITCHES-WIZARDS UNDERWATER

One of the works that are given to witches-wizards under the waters of the sea is to manage maternity centers in the village. When a woman comes to a maternity center for assistance to have a baby, a certain month would be chosen for the baby to be born or to die. But other months the babies would live. The answer to the problem of being barren, an agent is supposedly able to cure this childless condition by using the witchcraft powers of jujus. This form of witchcraft is considered the highest level.

If a barren woman goes to a native witch doctor, she would be asked to bring certain things such as human bones and ashes that were used to cook food for her. When she becomes pregnant and gives birth she does not deliver a normal human being. It could appear as a usual baby but it is a spiritually formed baby. In many women who are barren, the problems could be caused by demons. It is not a rare thing for a woman to be barren on earth but have children in the sea!

Some of the goods found in these maternity centers include eggs from the fetuses of pregnant women, human meat, flour made from human bones, bread made from human brains, peanuts from human teeth, vegetable oil from human bone marrow.

People receive curses and hardships into their lives and fall sick after eating such foods.

Some areas that people seek help by visiting a witch doctor are:

Material and financial prosperity
To succeed in one's job
To succeed in business, easy promotion
To succeed in school or university
To succeed in music industry
To become famous
To succeed in prostitution and attract rich clients
To succeed opposite sex
To succeed in marriage

THE POWER OF THE WIZARDS

In Africa, a middle-class wizard is considered to be a very powerful person. This means that if another person claims to be a witch or wizard and is not sharp, we can eliminate this individual. If you are not serving Jesus, the demons will try to kill you too. In the kingdom of the darkness, everyday witches and wizards try to test each other's power. If one wizard meets another person who claims to have supernatural powers, a wizard will want to see if that person is more forceful. This testing extends to Christians who say they have spiritual power. The way this power works is, a witch or wizard will fly and scan the Believers before they attempt to work their spells.

They do this because every witch or wizard knows that if a curse is sent upon a person and if the mission fails, the demons will return and use their powers upon the attacking wizard. In fact, the demons will bring ten more powerful new demons that will attack the wizard. Therefore, the wizard will send "scanning demons" to see if they can accomplish their attack before they attempt to strike. If the targeted person is living a holy life and is covered by the blood of Jesus, a wise wizard will not attack.

WITCHES' POTS

Every wizard is required to have a witch pot in which he must prepare human flesh for ritualism. Before I received Jesus, whenever

I needed a human sacrifice to work ritualism, I would turn myself into a crocodile and look for a swimmer in a lake, river or sea. This spiritualized crocodile would pull the person down under the water and then spew some kind of slime over the victim's body. Then the person would spring back to the top of the water. The victim would scream and thrash around in fear. The people with the victim would try to grab and try to hold on, but the oozy matter would stop them from being able to maintain their grip of the body. The body would slip from their grasp and sink again and again. Then the spiritual crocodile could pull the body up the water about fifty kilometers.

Afterward, I would take the body parts for my sacrifice. The people were busy looking in the area where they last saw the victim Several days later, the body would wash up somewhere else down the stream. In those days, if I, as a wizard, wanted to kill a person, I could look into their stomach and could see everything about them. Then spiritually, I would put my hand into their stomach and break their intestines. Then within the next twenty-five minutes the person would have a stomachache, pains. Soon, the situation would become very serious, and the person would die.

I had many spiritual eyes that Satan put around my head. I could see in all directions, front, back and sides at any time. A high level wizard has special weapons so that he can defeat his spiritual opponents.

STREET CHILDREN CAPTURED

Some children who have been captured by witches and wizards from the City Under the Sea can be rescued and converted. I personally have known many of these human children that have been converted to Christianity. In our church in Africa, we have children who have found the grace of God through salvation. We will tell them about Jesus but we will not let them receive Christ unless they bring their witches' pots and witchcraft boxes to the church. These pots and boxes are filled with sorcery, magical things, such as witches fetishes, charms, cross, powder, and "holy water." We destroy the demonic powers over these pots and articles through prayer in the Name of Jesus. In conclusion, it has been our experience that if we try to convert them without getting these articles, they will just return back to witchcraft. The witches will simply draw them back through the magical powers of the blood sacrifices conjured in their pots.

CHILDREN UNDER THE SEA

There are many children in the underwater city. Some of these children belong to witchcraft families. However many of these children are spiritual beings while others are hungry street children that have been captured by Satan's agents and turned to witchcraft. These are children who been abandoned by their parents and roam the streets. Sadly they are "throwaways" and prime candidates targeted by the witches/wizard to turn them into witches and wizards.

The queens of covens and the kings of wizards pick up street children. These poor children are fed potions of human flesh and drink human blood from their witches' pots. Soon they are captured, enslaved, and brought to the City Under the Sea to be trained as Satan's agents. Since these children are not born full blood into the craft, they can never rise to the leadership of the powers of darkness. However, they can be trained to be used as Satan's agents. Once they come to the underwater city, they go through initiation rites chanting and bathing them in blood, using both animal and human sacrifices. Here, human blood is used to appease the demigods. In exchange, they hope to be blessed by these gods with good fortune. They are given small pots, incense burners; special salts or herbs; bells or gongs; tribal drums; animal parts; bones; candles; incense; amulets; talismans; charms. They are taught to practice rituals, such as ESP powers, and talking to the spirits. They have a morbid fascination with the dead or with death. They mar their flesh with self mutilation. They have a fascination with blood, including cutting themselves or marking with tattoos or body paint.

These children will show unusual body movements and effects such as twitching, tics, rocking, glazed eyes, head banging, moaning or groaning, chanting. Lack of empathy toward the hurts in other people's lives. They act cruelly with inhumane acts against people and animals, or acts of vandalism. The demons tell them to give away meals to their relatives to gain demonic power over them. Of course they will put magical potions in these meals.

Many times these children are directed to work evil powers against their relatives, sometimes even bringing about death to them to prove their loyalty to Satan. These children are hardened in their hearts and they turn against their mothers, fathers, sisters, brothers and aunties to kill them.

It is a chilling story, but true. In Africa, we don't have kitchens in our churches as the churches in America do. The reason is that witches/wizards sometime try to use evil potions to draw weak people out of the church and into their arms. We are very protective concerning our Christian children.

These children that are trained under the sea by demons adopt a philosophy or attitude that shows a reversal of norms; for example, bad is good and good is bad. They have an animosity and cynicism toward Christianity, including God, Jesus Christ, the Bible, the church, pastors, youth leaders, and Christian ideals and ethics. Here is where homeless street children will be trained to become Satan's agents to steal souls. They are sent into churches to destroy them. Many well-meaning Christians cannot discern the evil nature of these children because they simply see them as children. Notwithstanding, the demons that use the bodies of these children to control them are shrewd. At the same time, these evil demons are under the control of Satan. The demons simply use the bodies of the children to rob, kill and destroy.

The sea children are able to cause great confusion and divisions among the church people. Some of the children from the City Under the Sea are used on the beaches to sell seashells to the tourists from all over the world. The unsuspecting buyer will take these shells home. The demons will attach themselves to these shells. This is a way that Satan can work powers through the shells as a point of contact. He uses them to destroy them and work evil in their homes. They can cause depression, loss of sleep, frequent nightmares, paranoia or excessive fear, restlessness.

I know a woman that took a beautiful shell from a child on the beach. She said his eyes had the sunken hollowed look that looked like black endless pools with largely dilated glassy pupils. Then she began to have sexual tormenting dreams. Suddenly, her yard filled with frogs. The Holy Spirit revealed to her to destroy the shell. She did and the dreams disappeared and so did the frogs.

Child witches and wizards can also be seen flying at night streaking like fiery rockets in the sky. Sometimes they can be seen whizzing through the night like fireworks. Midday is another dangerous time for a wizard, for then no man can cast a shadow. The superstition is that his soul has temporarily disappeared. A soul and shadow being equal, invisible spirits are looking for an abode. Children are forbidden to play with their shadows by candlelight lest they tie them in knots or lose them. These witchcraft-controlled children each have many snake spirits in their stomachs and these evil spirits are the mediums of their evil assignments.

One young boy, seven years old, recently appeared in our church. He had painted his shoes with the mixture of human blood from his victims and a red dye. He confessed that he was the king of wizards of his coven. He told our church that he had five snakes in his stomach, one red, one white, and three black ones. He said that he used these snakes to kill people for his sacrifices. I know that it is hard for a normal mind to believe these things, but I have him confessing this on videotape!

Another young girl came into the church. She was nine years old. She told us that she was the Queen of her coven. She told us that she was sent into the church to destroy it. I've personally seen many of these agents from under the water in other churches freely working without detection.

Here is an interesting Scripture in this context:

> Though they dig into Sheol, from there shall My hand take them: And though they ascend into heaven, From there shall I bring them down, And though they hide on the summit of Carmel, I will search them out and take them from there: and though they conceal themselves from My sight on the floor of the sea, from there I will command the serpent, and it will bite them… (Amos 9:2–3)

Here is a Scripture that connects the underworld compartment, Sheol, and the serpent in the bottom of the sea. It was a serpent in the Garden of Eden that ensnared Eve. This same creature is used in Revelation (20:2), as a description of Satan. The Scripture links sea serpents with Sheol, an underground abode of departed spirits. Even

"Sheol" (Hebrew) means "a place of inquiry," to bring fear into the hearts of men that they would repent "by the storms of life" to the gentle breeze of the Holy Spirit.

IS THE DEVIL REAL?

Even many Christians do not believe that Satan is real. They also do not believe in Hell. There is no fear of God and so they no longer bother praying for, or teach their children the Word. "And the great dragon was cast out, that old Serpent, called the Devil, and Satan, which deceiveth the whole world: he was cast out into the earth, and his angels were cast out with him" (Revelation 12:9).

I find it very interesting in today's world for anyone not to believe that Satan is very real and that he has targeted our children. As you look around, you can see that children are being attacked from every conceivable place possible.

Chapter Eight

Fantasy World

> **Wherefore thus saith the Lord GOD; Behold, I am against your pillows, wherewith ye there hunt the souls to make them fly, and I will tear them from your arms, and will let the souls go, even the souls that ye hunt to make them fly. (Ezekiel 13:20)**

ASTRAL TRAVEL

Frequently, occultists deeply desire to spend much of their time in a strange fantasy world. They can travel there through astral travel, in which their soul actually leaves their body to go into the next dimension. The Bible speaks to this fact most clearly. God describes Abraham's death in this manner when Abraham's spirit was released, and he died: "Then Abraham gave up the ghost, and died in a good old age, an old man, and full of years; and was gathered to his people" (Genesis 25:8). Of course, any person who practices astral travel is to a great depth demon possessed. A demonic spirit stays in the body to keep the human body alive while this diabolic practice happens. It is the demon's spirit maneuvering this witchcraft journey. Do not be deceived; this spiritual world is the supernatural world of the demonic. While in this dimension, the spirit of the person can be thoroughly deceived by the demonic host. While under demonic hypnotic control the child is given a counterfeit experience that makes him or her feel truly blessed and is very gratifying. The entire experience occurs in the supernatural (demonic) realm.

As I mentioned previously, the Devil gave me the power to fly. The Bible tells us about soul traveling by witches and wizards flying:

> And say, Thus saith the Lord GOD; Woe to the women that sew pillows to all armholes, and make kerchiefs upon the head of every stature to hunt souls! Will ye hunt the souls of my people, and will ye save the souls alive that come unto you? And will ye pollute me among my people for handfuls of barley and for pieces of bread, to slay the souls that should not die, and to save the souls alive that should not live, by your lying to my people that hear your lies? Wherefore thus saith the Lord GOD; Behold, I am against your pillows, wherewith ye there hunt the souls to make them fly, and I will tear them from your arms, and will let the souls go, even the souls that ye hunt to make them fly. Your kerchiefs also will I tear, and deliver my people out of your hand, and they shall be no more in your hand to be hunted; and ye shall know that I am the Lord. Because with lies ye have made the heart of the righteous sad, whom I have not made sad; and strengthened the hands of the wicked that he should not return from his wicked way, by promising him life: Therefore ye shall see no more vanity, nor divine divinations: for I will deliver my people out of your hand: and ye shall know that I am the Lord. (Ezekiel 13:18-23)

DEMONIC POWER

I had so much spiritual authority that many world leaders were placed under me spiritually. After my salvation experience, I promised God not to mention their names. When I saw them, I would flash a demonic sign with my fingers and they would smile and flash me a sign. I thought that I had all these powers but it was only after receiving Jesus that I discovered these powers had a hold over me.

Is the Devil real and do you believe that your children are in any danger? You need to pray that Jesus will open your eyes to see and how you can protect your children.

POWERS WORK

The people did not come from just the African coast. Influential people such as big businessman, doctors, lawyers and politicians were coming. I have seen important leaders come to the City Under the Sea such as Indians, Asians and Americans. These people were coming from all over the world, from everywhere. I even saw powerful political personalities in the underwater spirit world. These were people who had sold their souls for positions of power. They had given themselves over to greed and demon possession. They had sold their souls just to sit upon the seats of thrones of world tycoons, barons and kings. They came from all over the world. Some of the people who had been elevated to higher positions were given crowns and thrones. They were given titles such as, Queen of the West Coast or The King of the Wizards, etc. The devil's gods also had thrones.

At a tender age, I had been given these supernatural powers. I could fly (astral project—soul travel) and bring reports back to my father from the City Under the Sea. Once I was sent to represent my father in India, I didn't fly on the plane. I'd leave my soul and put other demons in this body to keep the body going. Then I was able to soul travel to anywhere in the world then, later on, return to Africa.

STRANGE GODS

This strange underwater habitation was used to manufacture things to lure people into busy lives so that they will not have time for God. Satan uses the gods of money, perversions, pornography, tattoos, piercing with rings and fashions. These demons also produce new inventions. There are also laboratories in which articles are invented to steal the souls of people one who foretells the future supernaturally. As a result, gadgets are dreamed up here before they ever appear in the world. For instance, I remember seeing personal computers there in the early seventies before they ever became popular in the world. Computers are exploding and will eventually replace the telephone and television. Moreover, the Internet is not regulated, so it is filled with evil music, pornography, witchcraft, and evil demonic game sites. So, it is Satan's playground. The Bible warns "Lay not up for yourselves treasures upon earth, where moth and rust doth corrupt, and where thieves break through and steal: but lay up for yourselves treasures in heaven…" (Matthew 6:19–20). It is window dressing for millions to stumble into wickedness. In any case, the computer is one of Satan's most powerful inventions to date.

Beneath the sea in the city, there are telescopes and televisions that seem to be supernatural. These machines are given to the agents to take into their homes for them to watch a person. These televisions allow agents to follow the movements of Christians and track the plans of churches that they are assigned to defeat.

Satan also invents new fashions there to ensnare souls. Think about the new fads such as body piercing, tattooing, electronics, extreme makeover, creams, perfumes, cosmetics, beautiful cars and fantasy things to steal people's souls. The Word of God warns, "For what shall it profit a man, if he shall gain the whole world, and lose his own soul?" (Mark 8:36).

If a person goes to a soothsayer, there is a written record that is kept under the sea. This curse of the law shown in the Bible will follow the person and their generational lines. Remember Satan has records!

RULED BY DEMONS

Though we were working with demons that we could feel, we were also being demonically controlled. We were like zombies ruled by evil demons. Now I can see that demons need human bodies to work through to accomplish their evil deeds.

Our motivations were void of human feelings. Our hearts were hard, cold as ice and full of horrendous hate. So people were to us like inanimate objects, like dead dolls. We were totally involved with our desires to progress to higher levels in this demonic world. As Satan's agents, it was sheer pleasure to wreak havoc upon and destroy the subjects of our assignments.

Our reason was Satan's malignant plots against mankind. We could cause all types of accidents, strife and wars between nations. We could use our powers to cause death, sickness, and discouragement and break up marriages. We would work through our magic television tracking systems to bring our enemies into bankruptcies. Backsliding Christians were marked for death, and we would quickly move to cause accidents to pull them into hell. Remember, the devil came to steal, kill and destroy.

Satan cannot appear to a person unless he owns them and they are slaves to serve him. At birth, God builds a supernatural wall of protection that divides people from Satan's realms. Once the person tears down the wall it is very hard to rebuild. On the other hand, Satan has permission to appear to them when they belong to him. Some demons appear as beautiful angels. They are full of deceptions and know how to disguise themselves as angels of light. Remember the Bible says that Beelzebub is called the prince of demons. He is the demon that controls all kinds of witchcraft. I have worked with this demon before. He doesn't go through the powers and principalities because he reports and is only responsible to Lucifer alone. Beelzebub, the lord of the flies, is in charge of the witches and wizards. He is the embodiment of cruelty.

WATER SPIRITS

The under the sea city has many gods. They have been worshiped since the beginning of time. I saw the forms of these gods. The pantheon of the gods and goddesses of Egypt included the forms of beings such as Bast, the cat goddess. She is the goddess of pleasure. The famed Isis is known to use her powers to heal humankind. Ma'at a goddess of law truth and justice while Seth is considered the god of chaotic forces. Serpent-headed Nehebka presided over funeral rites, Ibis-headed Throth is the god of the moon and Jezebel, the territorial goddess that captures the hearts of men and turns them away from their faith to draw them to her Baal.

In the demonic realms, demons work like the military. Each person under the sea has a master demon. He is a supervisor. If I had a question, like, why are we killing? Once my supervisor answered something like this, "It is in the Bible, and the man says that unless you eat his flesh and drink His blood, you will not live." We didn't know anything about the Bible. So we started eating human flesh and human blood so that we could live.

Some of the demons told me things that I could not understand until I was saved and delivered.

I remember one time that I asked a demon, "What is our reward for all the killing that we are required to do for Satan?"

The demon replied, "If you want a reward, there was a Man who came into this world. He spent only thirty-three years. He died. The people crucified Him. He died and on the third day, He arose from the dead."

I asked, "Who is this Man?"

The demon replied, "We cannot mention His name here."

I asked the demon. "Is it Mohammed?"

He said, "No man."

"Is it the Buddha?"

"No man, it is not the Buddha."

He said, "If you want a good reward, repent. We cannot repent, but you a human, created in the image of God still have chance. There was a Man who came into this world. He spent only thirty-three years. He was crucified, died, buried, and on the third day, He was raised from the dead."

I said, "Mention the name to me."

The demon said, "Shah! We cannot mention the name."

I said, "There is someone more powerful than our people?"

He said, "Oh, a hundred times."

I started mentioning principalities.

He replied, "A hundred times."

I asked him if there was somebody more powerful than Guru? (We called Satan Guru).

"More than ten times" the demon replied.

"Who is that person?" I questioned him.

He told me, "The people who follow this Man that I am talking about, we call them rebellious people."

He told me that if you go and follow that man, you would not suffer. I didn't know whom this demon was talking about, because he said that he was forbidden to say the man's name.

SPIRITUAL WATER SCENES

I remember that one of my favorite gods that I met in the underworld city was Mammon—the spirit of gold. He is made of a gold-type substance and has one eye at the center of his forehead and marks on his head. He is the world's most evil golden creature. He stands about eight feet tall. He walks like he has springs on his feet. He is a netherworld giant demigod, the spirit behind the money of the world. He rules in the lives of those dedicated to his name. He is in charge of Satan's storehouse of money. He has his hands in every evil thing on the earth. He is very powerful and worshiped by those who want to rule the world.

Mammon told me, "They are all joining Satan's plan for a New World Government because of their greed for filthy lucre. Passion, the lusts for riches are the roots of all evil." His dark eyes darted greedily back and forth.

"You're right about that," I sighed.

"Money makes the world spin." He turned again and looked straight through me. Then he talked about the statue of Zeus that has place in the entrance hall of the United Nations. He suddenly started laughing.

"Imagine this. He is the god of wars. Yet there he is, guarding the place where those dumb humans speak of peace and safety, and are supposed to rule over the peace of the world."

Then he asked me, "Do you like Zeus more than you do me?" his voice sounding jealous and whiny.

"No, of course not," I said. But on the spur of the moment, he had disappeared.

The information that I am telling you it is not a fairy tale, it is something that I have seen. You just don't know how privileged you are Christians. The Bible says the devils believe and tremble. It is true. The demons told me that Christians don't believe that there is a problem. They believe that many are under deception and unbelief.

Chapter Nine

Sea Giants

And every creature which is in heaven, and on the earth, and under the earth, and such as are in the sea, and all that are in them, heard I saying, Blessing, and honour, and glory, and power, be unto him that sitteth upon the throne, and unto the Lamb for ever and ever. (Revelation 5:13)

SEA BEHEMOTHS

I saw sea monsters, and later I discovered these very monsters described in the Bible. It is strange how Satan has blinded the eyes of church people concerning these beings in the sea.

The Bible shows that sea monsters are demons that appear as great mystifying beings that live under the sea. Look at how the Bible describes Leviathan King of the Sea. "In that day the Lord with his sore and great and strong sword shall punish Leviathan the piercing serpent, even Leviathan that crooked serpent; and he shall slay the dragon that is in the sea" (Isaiah 27:1).

The word dragon is the common Hebrew word for any large sea serpent. The word refers to Leviathan (Isaiah 27:1) and to Rahab as Egypt (Isaiah 51:9). The word dragon occurs fourteen times in the Old Testament and is translated as "sea monster" "serpent" or "dragon." It refers to any large sea or marine creature that is monstrous or hideous —good or bad—including the "sea monsters" God created in Genesis 1:21. The smaller creatures of the sea are called "living creatures" and "fish."

The Bible says, "So is this great and wide sea, wherein are things creeping innumerable, both small and great beasts. There go the ships: there is that leviathan, whom thou hast made to play therein" (Psalm 104:25-26). (See also Job 3–8.) "In that day the Lord… shall slay the dragon that is in the sea" (Isaiah 27:1) "In that day" refers to end time.

As a matter of fact, there are many mysteries in the sea. The sea also serves many purposes. The Bible says that sea monsters are real! There are spiritual entities under the sea that shape shifts (change) into many different forms and physical appearances of monsters, grotesque mutations that look like prehistoric creatures!

One proof text is found in the book of Revelation. There is a vision of the dragon, the beast and the false prophet, and from each of their mouths there comes, "unclean spirits like frogs…" (Revelation 16:13). Then we discover that the other powerful agency of evil in the Revelation, Babylon, is under the same influence. We see that this symbol of affluence, "is become the habitation of devils, and the hold of every foul spirit, and a cage of every unclean and hateful bird." (Revelation 18: 2).

In the search for wisdom the question is asked

> But where shall wisdom be found? and where is the place of understanding?…The depth saith, It is not in me: and the sea saith, It is not with me… Destruction and death say, We have heard the fame thereof with our ears. God understandeth the way thereof, and he knoweth the place thereof. For he looketh to the ends of the earth, and seeth under the whole heaven; To make the weight for the winds; and he weigheth the waters by measure. When he made a decree for the rain, and a way for the lightning of the thunder: Then did he see it, and declare it; he prepared it, yea, and searched it out. (Job 28:12, 14, 22–27)

Job finally finds wisdom and the "place of understanding" and to man he said, "Behold, the fear of the Lord, that is wisdom; and to depart from evil is understanding" (Job 28:28).

Since the "fear of the Lord is wisdom," then it stands to reason that those in the nether world of departed spirits do not have wisdom (they are represented by the "sea, "deep," "Abaddon," and "Death"). Abaddon is a large-scale supernatural being that personifies destruction. He is currently bound in Sheol-Hades. He is the diabolical king of the demons centaurs that will be released during the fifth trumpet judgment of Revelation 9.

The Full Gospel is a balanced Gospel, which includes the methods of the ministry of Jesus. He pointed His Church in the right direction when he said, "The spirit of the Lord is upon me because he hath anointed me to preach the gospel to the poor; he hath sent me to heal the brokenhearted, to preach deliverance to the captives, and recovering of sight to the blind, to set at liberty them that are bruised" (Luke 4:18).

A great percentage of Jesus' ministries were deliverance. "And he preached in their synagogues through all Galilee, and cast out devils" (Mark 1:39).

Jesus cast devils out! Jesus is our example! The Church has largely abdicated its authority and blandly disbelieves in such things. The enemy has come in like a flood, and few have resisted it.

MYSTERIES OF THE SEA

The mysterious book by David H. Lewis (author of *Mysteries of the Pyramid*) was located in fall of 2000. He gives testimony in this book that has been scanned and is available for the first time in many years, in both a comb-bound edition and perfect bound.

The author, having spent countless months searching through hieroglyphics, Naval records, ancient scrolled manuscripts, and ships logging, now brings to light one more haunting phenomenon from the archives of an explorer's heritage. It has long been a seaman's nightmare that demons possess many areas of our ocean, with concentrated thought aimed at our Bermuda Triangle and the mysterious disappearances occurring over these hundreds of centuries.

Vanished ships and planes of our present era have been documented as well as those collected over the past decade. Eerie and mysterious lights from the depths of the Atlantic were noticed by oceanic travelers and explorers for countless centuries, but more recently noticed and spasmodically recorded since Columbus's crossing in 1492.

Documented accountings from deep sea divers, Bathscape explorers, and oceanographers lay claim that depth soundings indicate a giant raised plateau buried far beneath the surface, that stretches from the west coast of Africa to the eastern coast of Bimini and the islands of Bermuda, is that of Atlantis, and remains active.

Logs clearly indicate many strange and frightening experiences that have baffled scientists for more than a decade. Many reports intimate light beams piercing the surface from great depths, lights near the surface that pass with speeds exceeding 200 knots, phosphorescent fog banks that engulf a ship or plane minutes before vanishing, unusual lights from a dome shaped objects within the ocean's sediment, and glowing rays that raise ships or yachts out of the water.

Lewis's book is designed to enlighten you on these mysteries, yet it does not solve all occurring phenomena of our oceans. There are however, strong indications that "Cities of the Deep" have existed before the chaos of Atlantis and are still continuing their activities into our present dates.

Chapter Ten

The Wizard's Power

Ye are of God, little children, and have overcome them: because greater is He that is in you, than he that is in the world. (1 John 4:4)

PAGANISM AND NATURE GODS

To many Africans, their god is one of his many manifestations. There are more than two hundred principal descriptive names. He is called by one of his many names ranging form "The Everlasting-One of the Forest" to "He who roars so loud that the Nations are Struck With Terror." His priests (medicine men and witch doctors) are recognized leaders of the tribal community.

The good news is that the gods of pagan Africa are not more powerful than the God of the Bible. Still there are many in Africa, and are many that worship the serpents. The Reverend T. L. Osborne tells the story that his wife went to Dohomny in Africa to set up a meeting. At a nearby serpent temple a priest had a huge snake around his head and body.

He told Daisy, "This is our god!"

She demanded, "Give me that snake." She took the snake from his hands and it instantly became as straight as a pole as if petrified. She turned to a trembling native preacher who was with her and said, "Take it!"

He obeyed. The snake was still like a pole. She took it back and handed it to the priest and immediately the serpent went almost wild and struggling as it wrapped itself around the priest.

Daisy said, "My God made all creation and we are not afraid of your snake god."

Praise God for brave Christian women like Daisy who obeyed the call of God. They have been followed by thousands of evangelists who have penetrated into every corner of Africa within the last hundred years. Today, through churches, chapels, mission schools and hospitals, the Africans are in daily contact with Christianity in its practical form.

UNSEEN WORLD

I tell you that the spiritual realms are certainly real! Beyond the veil of the flesh there is a world unseen by human eyes, a world seen only when the eyes of one's spirit are opened. It is a world more real than this physical world. It existed before the world was formed, even before man first appeared on earth. Behind this veil is the world of evil spirits. Although they are invisible, they are forceful and their work does affect the world as their powers are transferred into the physical realms. Know this. There truly is a satanic world conspiracy, so vast and terrible, that the human mind cannot conceive it. This treacherous demonic movement is real. The forces of evil move tirelessly to bring their kingdom of the Antichrist and with him darkness unlike any the world has ever seen before into power. They use human beings as agents to enforce their evil wills to influence the souls of men and women. Millions upon millions will follow this ungodly world scheme of the Devil. These spirits use objects and symbols to draw humans into their world of spiritual blindness.

NEW WORLD COMING

I have worked with these devils, also called demons, dark angels and foul evil spirits. I know them and understand how they operate. They are literally ransacking the earth today and possessing the souls of untold thousands of people. I have personally attended world conferences and heard the Devil's plans to rule the world. His New Age Religion requires a full-fledged worship of Satan. I remember his conversation with a demon at one of these conferences.

He mentioned, "One of these days some great leader that will be respected by the world as a man of peace. He will settle the Arab-Israeli dispute. Watch out when this happens, for he will be the Christ.

His sweet words of peace will soon lead to the most ravaging seven years of terror the world has ever witnessed. Then we will win."

He told us. "The world's new religious leaders are committed to ushering in this New World Order."

We hoped that it would come soon. We were committed to bring in peace, love and brotherhood under the leadership of the New Age Christ (not Jesus Christ). We believed Satan's lies that whenever he ruled the world, things would be better. Also, we had worked so hard to be the spiritual leaders of the world. He already possessed numerous world leaders with his Ascended Masters (demons) to control nations. At the same time they were planning and working especially inside Christian Churches. Luciferin doctrines were steadily being introduced and, in many cases, warmly embraced by evangelists, pastors, and millions of ordinary Christians in the pews.

Strange as this may seem, some of these leaders were frightened by our presence in these planning world conferences. They recognized that our witchcraft powers were real. They had witnessed our reports of great destruction and were aware that if Satan commanded us, we could kill them.

Satan was using many witches and wizards to destroy his enemies' incredibility, and he has filled many world-known religious leaders with wicked spirits to declare his false prophecies. Soon, the entire world will be under these mad men through the coming international new world. His conquering armies will ravage Asia and Europe in a merciless campaign of bloodletting and terror never seen before in the history of mankind. As a result, the swarm of evil will invade the nations around the entire globe. In fact, we were told that innumerable evil spirits' purposes were to prepare all mankind to rebel against God. They have been working since the beginning to usher in Satan's kingdom. They have used many methods to reach their goals.

The evil spirits work through such things as horror movies heavy metal rock music, sci-fi television stories. They achieve their objectives by attacking the youth and family structure. These demons cause strife, rebellion and divisions. They attack the male leadership in the family to cause disrespect for authority. They fill the minds of the people with lies and sexual gratification, spellbinding them with greed. Satan has been desensitizing them to horror, murder, and acts of violence, and debauchery. He has used the media to mock the ministers of the Gospel by using negative images on the television.

He uses every means of attack, the arts, the media, the corruption of influential leaders and the depraving of the human race to speed up his agenda. The world has begun to crave the supernatural and popular television shows that highlight mystic powers. Demon powers and rulers of darkness to completely rule the world economic, political, and religious systems set the world stage.

They are ready to receive these great appearances. Believe me. They will adore the Great Master. You may ask, "Who is this Great Master?" You can find a picture of Antichrist when he comes to his place of absolute power and of rebellion, in Daniel Seven and Eleven. In these passages, we see the Antichrist magnifying himself above the true God and all the gods' men have historically worshiped, having no regard for established religions, and promoting the worship of him. He will be called the god of fortresses and will engage in religious practices of a superstitious nature. There truly is a raging battle for the soul of the world.

Evil spirits are engaging in relentless battles that are fighting against opposing forces. These conflicts are exploding against the entire human race. Principalities and powers, world rulers of darkness, wicked spirits in high places and an innumerable Numbers of evil spirits contemplate the destruction of mankind. These principalities and powers are opposing the whole human race as shown in (Ephesians 6:12).

It is true, behind the problems of the world and behind every evil, which manifests itself in mankind, there is a hierarchy of evil spirits, namely the devil and his angels in an organized kingdom influencing this present world. These powers are at various levels of authority that sit as world rulers of the present darkness, wicked spirit in high places.

Just as the Bible warns us, there will be wars and rumors of wars, and famine and pestilence will soon follow. The beginnings of sorrows have already begun in certain parts of the world. I know about the power of these conquering spirits. I was there with them. I know their tactics. I know how they work on governments, cities, and churches.

The Bible shows that the devil always seeks to pollute and destroy the head, the leader, the king, and the priest. It was not the misfits and the confirmed defeatists, but the emperor on his throne that were given over to all forms of demon manifestations and worship that were inspired by Satan.

The Scripture says, "Then the king commanded to call the magicians, and the astrologers, and the sorcerers, and the Chaldeans, for to shew the king his dreams. So they came and stood before the king" (Daniel 2:2).

The Bible is right, what the Bible says in the books of Daniel and Revelation will soon come to pass. Chaos will reign. Demons of lawlessness and rebellion will rage in the nations on the earth. Planned nuclear weapons will rain hell on the people of the world. The forces of an evil holocaust will prevail and clash against all of mankind for a final time.

The puzzle is almost completely in place; the masses of the world are still operating in the old world order. Many cannot see what terrible disasters are soon to come. It is being done before their eyes but they cannot see a thing. The bewitching-blinding spirits have closed their eyes and concentrated their minds on foolish things. The Holy Scripture says that Jesus Christ wins the battle of the worlds final conflict, but I tell you that Satan believes that he will be successful.

THE PLAN

Look at the astonishing scripture in (Revelation 13:1–10), that reveals the destination of the Beast. John "in the spirit," finds himself stationed on the sands of the sea—that same great sea upon which Daniel beheld the winds striving in their fury. He becomes aware of a monstrous Beast rising out of the troubled elements. He sees horns emerging, and the number of them is ten, and on each horn a crown. He sees the heads that bear the horns, and these heads are seven, and on the heads are names of blasphemy. Presently the whole figure of the monster is before him. Its appearance is like a leopard or panther, but its feet are as the feet of a bear, and its mouth as the mouth of a lion. He saw also that the Beast had a throne, and power, and great authority. One of his heads showed marks of having been fatally wounded and slain, but the death stroke was healed. He saw also the whole earth wondering after the Beast, amazed at its majesty and power, exclaiming at the impossibility of withstanding it, and celebrating its favorable position to everything.

He saw, and the Beast was speaking great and blasphemous things against God, blaspheming His name, His tabernacle, even them that dwell in heaven, assailing and overcoming the saints on earth, and wielding authority over every tribe, and people, and tongue, and nations. He saw all the dwellers upon earth, whose names are not written in the book of life of the Lamb slain, did worship this Beast. And for forty-two months the monster holds its place and enacts its resistless will. This is the picture of the monstrous Beast of the sea. He comes out of the agitated sea to become an all-important player in the end times.

I remember that in the early 70s we had a world conference. Satan was on the throne. He was receiving worship from every being present. Their voices were lifted in chanting and they were bowing to the ground. The world occultists in higher positions from America and from all over the world were there. Nominal Christians were invited. In fact everyone is invited to the New World Brotherhood except real Christians. Their leaders were simply excluded from all planning sessions. To Guru (this is what we called Satan) real born again Christians were like a bunch of pest-cockroaches.

Guru told us "our testimonial has been developed for the revival of Satan worship that has pierced the continent of Europe and the rest of the globe. The spiritual battle is now out in the open even more, with our forces daring to present bizarre activity around the world."

It was true. We have seen that Satanism is spreading like a cancer, in ways that only a generation ago would have been considered impossible. It has raced into the West from hippies holding witchcraft discussions to dogs being sacrificed and their blood being drunk at Satan worshiping ceremonies, and fire walking carried out as a part of the ritual. In initiation ceremonies, new recruits are required to eat the entrails of an animal while its heart still beating.

An ethereal glow came from within Guru if he heard something that agreed with his ideas. He seemed to be very excited concerning his progress but then he turned his attention to the Christians. He said, "I want to get those rebellious people" (he called Christians rebellious people).

The Bible says there will soon be a widespread falling-away as we receive the power of ruling the world.

He asked, "How can we get them to come to our side?"

There is a demon in charge of fashion, called Moloch. Moloch has a face, breast, and female organ. Another demon called a Marine Demon is half fish, half woman with flying hair.

These demons said, "we can get into the rebellious Christians through fashion."

"Do you really believe this is going to work?" One of the world leaders asked.

Guru replied, "Picture this, the heads of the Catholic and Greek churches, Jews and Muslims, Christian bishops and cardinals, snake handlers, Satanists and witches, all meeting for the first time under one roof. Imagine this. The delegates make enchanting speeches about peace and unity and they will read passages from their various religious books and recite their particular prayers to their gods for world peace."

"Yes," Mammon countered, "meanwhile, think about this, our money is creating the New World Order at such a rapid pace. Everyone is standing in line, taking the big bucks, to be deceived. It's like taking candy from a baby."

He seemed to be invigorated by the approaching darkness of the night. There was always something new and powerful whenever the sun tumbled into obscurity. Some of the areas that demons are powerfully working are: demon inspired religions and books: Sorcery, divination, Ouija boards, fortune telling, voodoo, ESP, Satan worship, spiritualism, parapsychology, numerology, fetishes, table-tipping, Tarot Cards, clairvoyance, Great Seal, alchemy, talismans, tea leaves, telepathy, New Age, witchcraft, astrology, black arts, materializations, levitation, Yoga, palmistry, scientology, white magic, colorology, black mass, phrenology, I Ching, Kabala, automatic writing, clairaudience, pendulum healing, psychic portraits, crystal gazing dream analysis, Rosicrucians, Devil's pentagrams, Yoga meditation, reincarnation, personal programming, astral projection, Transcendental Meditations, Channeling, Secret Societies, Martial Arts, Karate and many more.

We know that for some strange reason, a wizard or witch couldn't destroy committed Christians. The witch or wizard must find a way to cause the Christian to sin. If a Christian commits a sin, and doesn't repent, then a witch/wizard will lead the person to sin again. Then the hedge that is around the Christian will begin to crack. Then gradually—gradually and finally, the witch/wizard will have access to that Christian and will kill that person. The Bible says that the wages of sin are death.

SPIRITUAL BEINGS

A person must have spiritual eyes to tell the differences between demons and the human being spirits in the sea. Some of the demons in the bottom of the sea appear in the forms as humans while others proudly sport their fallen natures and appear as gods and goddesses. Some come out as angels of light, while others look like mythical monsters. In fact, you can see the shapes and forms of some of these monsters by going into rock and roll record shops and viewing some of the covers on the CDs as they have revealed themselves to the artists. Also, they have exposed themselves to many people who are inventing demonic computer games. Another promoter is the horror movie. I must warn the reader that you cannot walk away clean when you expose yourself to Satan's demonic fantasy world. These unclean spirits attach themselves to these demonic articles. Then, they will enter into your house and then into your body. Believe me, after exposure, you will be tormented unless you are fortunate enough to receive Jesus Christ and deliverance.

Chapter Eleven

Satan's Agents

For rebellion is as the sin of witchcraft, and stubbornness is as iniquity and idolatry. Because thou hast rejected the word of the Lord, he hath also rejected thee from being king. (1Samuel 15:23)

SATAN'S HUMAN AGENTS

Apart from demons, he has human agents. They monitor the new Christian. The agent will say, "brother, sister, I'm taking care of you."

Words are spirit. The words may not sound evil but they will be spoken under the inspiration of a devil. The agent will speak the words to deceive. Remember the divination woman in Acts 16:16-18: "And it came to pass, as we went to prayer, a certain damsel possessed with a spirit of divination met us, which brought her masters much gain by soothsaying: The same followed Paul and us, and cried, saying, 'These men are the servants of the most high God, which shew unto us the way of Salvation.' And this did she many days. But Paul, being grieved, turned and said to the spirit, 'I command thee in the name of Jesus Christ to come out of her.' And he came out the same hour." The words she spoke were true. However, the Apostle discerned the spirit behind the words and did not receive the words spoken by the soothsayer. He rebuked her publicly so that the Christians that she was trying to deceive would not accept them either.

For instance, if the agent knows that the Christian has a love of money, he will say something such as, "Oh, I have business. We are going to get fifty thousand dollars." These words are innocent sounding. However, because the words are coming from the demonic realms, it has some power. So these words will enter into the Christian's spirit and get control of that person's soul. Within a year or two, the demon has grown, so the Christian will be looking for a way and means to grab money —because it is money, instead of serving Jesus. This is why the Bible tells us to have no fellowship with an unbeliever. If in the Christian's past he was a drinker, he will say we have wine that has no alcohol—taste it. Now because it is a demonic person, as soon as it touches the lips, it is polluted. Spiritually, the Christian will put alcohol inside. Though this is not alcohol that person will have the same sensations as if they had drunk alcohol. They will enjoy the pleasures just as though they were actually drinking the real wine. That person will keep on and then one day the demons will remove magic and it will be like water. Then the Christian will crave real alcohol and go for wine with alcohol.

These demons and agents will work on a Christian for years. This is why the Apostle Paul said, "Be careful that you do not fall." They work on people for a long time. The Bible says, "My people perish for a lack of knowledge," (Hosea 4:6).

HOW WIZARDS DRAW CHRISTIANS TO BACKSLIDE

When indulging in witchcraft, I was an absolute spiritual slave. The agents that live mostly in the sea are ardent haters of Christianity. They will go to great lengths to war against the Church of Jesus Christ. Believers are the targets. Guru had venomous hatred for God and His people. He told us that the reason that he hated God was because he drove him out of his place. His hatred seems to saturate us with the same spirit. He was hungry for souls and our jobs were to get them for him.

Former witches and wizards have given many testimonies that they are taught to go into Christian churches and pretend to be Christians so that they can destroy the ministry. I know for a fact that Satan will lead a person into the church of Jesus Christ for the sole purpose of destroying the leadership.

Our targets were to seek out sincere Christians to tempt them to sin. He vocalized that hypocrites were already subjects of his kingdom and how they are used to make weak Christians fall. He continued to instruct us that we should only fight born again Christians because all the other people in the world belonged to him! The name of Jesus was never mentioned in this underwater city.

In the demonic world, the very day that a Christian gives his or her life to Jesus as Lord and Savior, the demons mark the first day of the fifty-two days—they have seven times in a cycle which is fifty two days after fifty-two days, then they will form another cycle and will release two demons and about two hundred or three hundred evil spirits to track that person. In the beginning when the person accepts Jesus, they are so zealous and on fire. The demons will not come near because the person is so powerful.

After a time, these demons will begin to recall the person's past. When they want to read the Word, they speak to his/her mind, the sins that they loved. If a person is a smoker and has not stopped, a doper and has not stopped, the demons will use these open spiritual doors to draw him back. They will distract the person and stir up his flesh to desire every sin of the past again. If a person has not gone through deliverance, the sins of the flesh still control him. Then the demons will work to draw him back.

Later on, they will just trail the person for five, ten years. Because the Christian was previously with the devil, he knows them. He will begin to dwell on their past by projecting these images upon their minds or in their dreams. The demons cannot get the Christian for the first five years, but at six years, they began to work against the person's zeal. They will use little demons to bring to the people's self-esteem, laziness, and coldness toward attending church. The demons have time. They will work these little things gradually. If the Christian accepts the demon's idea into their minds, soon the demons will be able to lead them away from God.

DISCERNING SPIRITS

The Bible says, "And if it seem evil unto you to serve the Lord, choose you this day whom ye will serve; whether the gods which your fathers served that were on the other side of the blood, or the gods of the Amorites, in whose land ye dwell; but as for me and my house we will serve the Lord" (Joshua 24:15).

One of the most important tools in the Church is to be able to discern and cast out evil spirits when they are operating within the

Church. We are not supposed to cast out the people, only the evil spirits! "Be not deceived; God is not mocked: for whatsoever a man soweth, that shall he also reap" (Galatians 6:7). The occult is defined as secretive-hidden knowledge or wisdom beyond human understanding. It could also be described as supernatural perception from sources other than God. "The secret things (hidden knowledge) belong to the Lord our God: but those things which are revealed belong unto us" (Deuteronomy 29:29).

The Bible declares deliverance for all men through Jesus Christ. "For God sent not His son into the world to condemn the world but that the world through Him might be saved and to preach deliverance to the captives and recovering of sight to the blind, to set at liberty them that are bruised" (Luke 4:18).

If Jesus does not really occupy the highest place in our hearts, controlling all, something else does—millions are now serving other gods. "For thou shalt worship no other god: for the Lord, whose name is Jealous, is a jealous God." (Exodus 34:14).

There are only two sources for supernatural power: Jesus or Satan and seeking power beyond the Word of God and Jesus Christ finds one stepping into the world of the Occult. Witchcraft is very religious, and the people that are seeking this evil power hope to find in it as a reason for their existence and to fill a void in their soul. Instead, they will enter a door that very few are able to exit. Once ensnared by the Devil, the person's mind, body and spirit is totally bound by the powers of darkness. The only way out is through the grace of God and the Blood of Jesus Christ!

ONLY CHRISTIANS HAVE POWERS TO CAST OUT DEVILS

I have seen how demons possess and work through the bodies of sorcerers, witches, enchantresses, magicians, and the wizards. Evil spirits can identify individuals and discriminate against them. Only Christians have the spiritual authority to cast out devils. The spirits discerned the spiritual state of the Sons of Sceva: "Jesus I know, and Paul I know, but who are you?" they asked the sons of Sceva (Acts 19: 15).

The truth is that demons can surely recognize the spiritual authority of a child of God, and they must yield to the superior power of the Kingdom of Jesus Christ. These sons of Sceva (Jewish Exorcist) had attempted to cast demons out of a demonized man "by Jesus whom Paul preacheth ... And the man in whom the evil spirit was leaped on them and overcame them" (Acts 19:16). The sons of Sceva were not believers in Jesus Christ and therefore they had no spiritual authority over demons because they belonged to the same kingdom of Satan. The demons know true believers and must honor the name of Jesus.

Ephesus, as this incident shows, was famous in antiquity as a center for magic, sorcery, witchcraft, and the like, which sought knowledge of the future and personal control of events by the supernatural help of spirits, which was widespread throughout the ancient Mediterranean world. Some who use these magical arts, sorcery, and witchcraft were not malicious. They only intended to cause personal well being and to ward off evil spirits from the lives of people who believed that sudden illness or tragedy could happen to them. Other practices, however, aimed to carry out supernatural powers or evil spirits for personnel ends at others' expense or to harm other people. No matter what people's intentions are, their actions put them in contact with demons.

WIZARDRY

I know how the demons operate because these same demons possessed my body (I was a wizard). I know the demons by their names and their nature. They taught me how to use charms and to wear amulets for protection. I made love potions to drink. I uttered ancient witchcraft incantations to bind spirits to certain actions. I cast spells and cursed tablets to bring disaster to my enemies. I summoned the spirits of the dead. I used all these and other means to help people who felt powerless before their unclear futures. When I commanded the spirits to do various things for me, including causing my enemies to die, they would obey. Naturally, I thought that I was controlling the devils, only to discover after becoming a Christian that they were, in fact, controlling me.

Demons do mental or physical work through people and use them as Satan's agents. They strive to inhabit human bodies. They work out their unspeakable lusts and evil longings. They have unlimited freedom to work through unbelievers. However, they do their most powerful work when they find a willing vessel such as a wizard or witch.

The word wizard is a term that points out a person who is mindful of the supernatural. It is a term that is also used as the masculine of witch or warlock. There are many versions of witchcraft practiced today; however, they all hold the same beliefs and practices. The spirit of witchcraft is destructive evil, wicked. A witch can assign a witchcraft spirit to operate on behalf of a person. We used to call it witchcraft contamination. A witch can contaminate a willing person by association.

They work through dreams. The person will have meetings. If a person dreams that someone is trying to put witchcraft upon him and he does nothing about it, within six months he will become a witch.

Biblical positions against magic, sorcery and witchcraft are very severe against practitioners, male and female, who use such practices to glorify themselves, to harm others and to manipulate the spirit world against the Spirit of God. In the Old Testament there are strong prohibitions against this sort of activity. For instance, in Exodus 22:18, the penalty for a sorcerer is death. Deuteronomy 18: 9-14, emphasizes that the Hebrew people are not to engage in divination, soothsaying, augury, sorcery, or consultation with the dead. They must be completely loyal to the Lord God. The terrifying effects of a consultation with the dead are described in 1 Samuel 28:3-25, as Saul consults a medium to bring up Samuel from the dead. The prophets too, urge the Hebrew people not to listen to soothsayers and other practitioners of the occult arts (Isaiah 2:6 and Jeremiah 27:8:11).

The New Testament assumes the existence of an extensive spirit world but shows that the Spirit of God manifest in Jesus and his apostles is triumphant over these spirits. The Gospel demonstrates that these spirits recognize and submit to Jesus in (Matthew 8:28–34, Mark 5:1–20, 9:14–29, Luke 4:31–37, 9:37–43, 11:14–26).

Then the Book of Acts provides four accounts showing the gospel's triumph over people who use spirits or are possessed by them. Simon Magus, with a wide following in Samara, is amazed by the power of the Holy Spirit and wants to buy the power of bestowing it (Acts 8:4–25). On Cyprus, a Jewish false prophet named Bar Jesus realizes that he will lose his power over his client, the Roman proconsul Sergius Paulus, if Paulus believes in Jesus (Acts 13:8-12).

In Philippi Paul expels the spirit of divination that recognized in the woman that Paul and Silas are "servants of the Most High God" with the result that her owners lose the money that can be earned by her divination (Acts 16:16-24). And finally, here in Ephesus, the seven sons of the Jewish high priest Sceva attempt to use the Name of Jesus without understanding the implications of it (Acts 19-11-20). These believers in the risen Christ know that the Spirit of God is more powerful than the force of evil and even death itself.

In Galatians Paul asks the church, "Who has bewitched you?" (Galatians 3:1). After receiving the Gospel that he had formerly preached to them of the crucified, risen Christ, these people had fallen under the spell of a bewitching spirit.

THE NATURE OF DEMONS

In the Bible the word wizard in Hebrew is *aid 'oni* , which is properly defined as "the knowing or the wise one." Like the "familiar spirit," Hebrew *Ob* it means first the alleged "spirit of a deceased person" (actually the divining demon). Then it came to mean him or her who divines by such a spirit or demon. Therefore, both terms mean the divining spirits and the medium through which the demon divines. The two concepts, "the divining spirit and "the divining mediums," are frequently so closely identified as to be thought of as one, as in (Leviticus 19:31 and 20:6).

Talking to the dead is absolutely forbidden by God. It is a superhuman knowledge of the spirit dwelling the human body that makes a medium a wizard. One of the means of seeking power is by the use of drugs the human brain is tormented and sometimes destroyed.

MAGICAL ARTS

Witches and wizards are taught to use incantations, potions, herbal concoctions and other magical arts to bring about curses. There are many testimonies of people who suffered and even died due to witchcraft curses sent against them. Demons inflict diseases because they can possess men and women, can possess animals, can oppose spiritual growth, and can disseminate false doctrines, and can torment people. Demons can talk or cry with a loud voice, using the tongues and lips of humans. They can tell lies and make people believe lies. They can even preach. They know the Scriptures but they twist the Word of God to suit their plans and to bewitch the minds of people. Although demons are spirits, they have memories, can stand, walk and seek rest when disembodied from a human being. They can tell fortunes, make people strip off their clothes, cause suicides, and render a person insane, or cause a body to be bowed in affliction. They can cause confusion, division, hate, anger, jealousy, pride, lust etc. They can drive a person into depression, despair, murder and suicide. They can oppress or possess a person.

I can tell you this that no wizard or witch in Africa could ever deny the reality of Guru (Satan). He used to appear to us sometimes as a handsome angelic being and other times as a hideous grotesque figure true to his wicked nature. There was no doubt in our minds that he existed. We heard his voice and saw him often enough. Guru told us that he had wrongfully been ejected from heaven but one day he would regain his rightful position to rule the universe, earth, the sky and the seas. Then the Christian church would be overthrown and vanquished. However before all this could happen, evil must increase, wickedness must grow—laws would have to be changed so that infidelity could prevail. Nothing is sacred in his plan absolutely nothing!

Chapter Twelve

The Deep Things of Satan

And the Lord said unto Satan, Behold, all that he hath is in thy power; only upon himself put not forth thine hand. So Satan went forth from the presence of the Lord. (Job 1:12)

SYNAGOGUE OF SATAN

The Bible refers to witchcraft as the "deep things of Satan," (Revelation 2:18–24), which refers to the Jezebel prophetess who leads members into practices of immorality and idolatry. We read of "the synagogue of Satan" (Revelation 2:9) at Pergamos was "even where Satan's seat is" (Revelation 2:12–13). From these Scriptures a person can be taught that a different Gospel, different Jesus, a different spirit is inspired by witchcraft.

Everything about Satan is the exact opposite of the Kingdom of God. The Bible is true. I know because I have seen the throne of Satan. It is made of what is sometimes called "fool's gold" because though it looks like real gold, it is not real. There is a background of darkness surrounded by stars, moon and sun. He has human skulls circling his throne. Desecrated candles made of human fat flicker from the center of a goat's head. The throne was engraved with snakes and dragons and flames and fire rose from his seat. His light was so bright that it almost blinded me. He is truly an angel of light.

I stood glued to the spot, unable to move—hypnotized. There were no seats there because when anyone worshiped Guru they prostrated themselves on the ground. I saw an effigy hanging on the wall of Lucifer, half man and half beast, with cloven feet. He had a proud look on his face. Another image reveals him as beautiful angel of light. In front was a high platform was an altar, on it were knives, cups and vessels made of fake gold. I saw a demon standing at his right hand with a flaming sword. I knew instantly this powerful demon was one of the "Ascended Masters." The new religious leaders of the world believe these are invisible "higher beings" and they claim to have ruled over the earth since the beginning of time. These New Agers teach that every so often one of these Ascended Masters will come as a great avatar (leader) to possess an individual to teach mankind some very important things that the world needs to know.

Then everyone was bowing before Guru's (Satan's) throne. Then everyone was bowing before Guru's (Satan's) throne raising their arms in worship. Everyone broke forth with wails and invocations to Guru, the great god of darkness, and death and mystery arose. The air was full with evil. His essence was wrapped in light so dazzling that I could hardly catch Guru's form.

An Ascended Master spoke, "We are going to summon the old gods Apollon or Apollyon, Abaddon or Apollo, depending upon whether you're Roman, Persian or Greek, they are not dead…they are helping us to build the New World Order and everyone will worship Guru. They believe these religious personalities, the Buddha, Iman, etc. were great avatar teachers.

"You are a part of the time when we are coming to take possession of all the leaders of the world to take charge of the New World Order…"

FALSE SIGNS & WONDERS

We can see that the Devil does inspire false signs and wonders and false prophecies in the Church. Since the Devil desires to control people's lives, he finds willing human agents who are filled with ambition for power to do his work. Then he sows his agents in the Church of Jesus Christ. Also, he has millions in the world that he uses to work evil powers, such as hexes, spells and animal and human blood sacrifices against the Church. Believe me, if a Christian Church or an individual Christian has an open door through hidden sin, these powers of destruction will be successful. His infiltrators that are sown in the church will usurp the authority of leadership and work in the background to catch people in a web of deceit. The Bible clearly shows these bewitching people serve other gods, and work with seducing spirits. Let us look at 1 Timothy 4:1–3:

> Now the Spirit speaketh expressly that in the latter times some shall depart from the faith, giving heed to seducing spirits, and doctrines of devils; Speaking lies in hypocrisy; having their conscience seared with a hot iron; Forbidding to marry, and commanding to abstain from meats, which God hath created to be received with Thanksgiving of them which believe and know the truth.

Remember this, Satan is helpless with his destructive powers unless there are open doors of sin that put a person in agreement with his power. His agents work through sensational attractions and fascinations by false prophets, false signs and wonders, etc., (Mark 13:22). People who are drawn away from the truth are shown to have seared consciences, (1 Timothy 4:1), deceived, (1 John 2:18, 26; 2 Timothy 3:13); fascination to evil ways, objects, or persons, (Proverbs 12:25) and/or seduced, enticed, (1 Timothy 4:1,2; 2 Timothy 3:13).

DIVINATION

The means of seduction are his agents' use of spirits of divination, psychology, New Age religions and sexual sins of adultery, fornication, pornography. This is worked through people who are inspired by the spirit of the Antichrist by their hunger for personal ambition. I have experience working in this invisible world of demons as one of his agents using Satan's power. I remember how the powers and principalities operate with their underlings. I know these things because I spent twelve years of my life in the City Under the Sea.

MYSTICISM

The word sorcerer from the Latin *sores,* "a lot," means one who throws or declares a "lot." It is like throwing dice. Sorcery functions in divination, having its connection with the demonic powers and idol worship. This art in ancient times was also practiced in connection with pharmacy or mixing of drugs into medical compounds for various healings. It also includes the entire field of witchcraft such as voodoo, wizardry, black magic, soothsaying and mysticism. A wizard or witch must submit not only his soul, body and spirit to the Devil but also his family (if married) to be used as tools and vessels to Satan at his discretion. Based upon initiations ceremonies and oaths, creeds, and vows made, Satan has every legal right to use (or dispose of) the person or any member of his family for his purposes. This really gives insight into the power and control that the Devil has over his followers.

The supposed distinction between white (good) and black (evil) is clear throughout Africa. The former is believed to be helpful and protective and falls within the sphere of the medicine man who prepares healing potions and of the witch doctor that wages war on witches; the latter are the monopoly of wizards' sorcerers.

White magic tackles the problems of disease, both physical and mental, of accidents and misfortunes, and of natural disasters like drought. It works in the open, in the light of day, and nearly always entails a public ceremony. Black magic is black because the practitioner, man or woman, works in the dark. Actually all magic I evil both black and white.

Sudden death from sheer terror is known in cases where a man discovers an evil fetish like a cracked bone secreted by a wizard in his house; or sees a trail of powder laid around his hut; or finds a clay image of himself pinned down with pegs and pierced with thorns in the head and heart. The psychological effect of such methods is not hard to assess. For where such evil objects are being used against a man, obviously the intention is evil and he is therefore in grave danger.

DIABOLICAL ENDS

In Africa no witch or wizard sees that witchcraft as good. They know the source. They do talk in terms of "white witchcraft" and "black witchcraft" and they do not practice so-called "white witchcraft" as it is practiced in America. Witchcraft is witchcraft. They know that the Devil is not good—even though he may pretend to be good—he is evil. To accept the premise of something called white witchcraft suggests that white magic is beneficial in nature, is to say that there is a godly side to the Devil. He uses witchcraft to accomplish his diabolical ends. He leads uninformed people into a life of occult spiritual bondage. Trudge into his territory of supernatural practices, and the person runs the risk of achieving Satan's ends. African wizards and witches know that they are possessed by supernatural powers of darkness because they have a pact made with the devil or a familiar spirit.

I have often witnessed deep rivalry and hatred between people practicing the black arts. There are those who boast of great power. These people are always testing each other's power. Some more powerful witches and wizards can stop other less powerful witches. There is a constant war over who controls and possesses the most power. It is ruthless with absolutely no regard for the sanctity of life.

Africans base their fear of witches on the argument that somebody—some person or spirit—has to be responsible for the inexplicable. When, for instance, should one man be struck down by lightning and another spared, especially if the dead man is a good hunter, a loving husband, and a kind father? The African calls this incident witchcraft. For witches, although they are mortal, have supernatural powers that they invariably use to harm, never to benefit their neighbors. A few of them are men—wizards or warlocks, but the majority are women. An African witch can be young, because her evil power and activities have nothing to do with her age or appearance.

In fact, there is not much she can do about her inherent wickedness, though if she is lucky her supernatural powers will be quiescent and she will be able to live a normal life as a member of her community. But if she is an active witch she will be bound to use her evil powers until she is caught by the witch doctor.

A witch or wizard invariably practices her/his activities at night. Then she/he leaves the body and flies off, sometimes as a ball of fire, sometimes as a night bird, to the tops of trees or secret groves. The witches convene in these places for their nocturnal orgies. These orgies take the form of cannibalism for witches feed on human flesh and are especially partial to the meat of babies and young children.

The flesh eating however seems to be regarded by many Africans as a mystical rite, devouring of the "soul" of the victim, hence the slow withering away of his actual body. The witch doctor must hasten to identify the witch before she figuratively consumes a vital organ like the heart, lungs or liver. Consequently if he catches the witch and proves her guilt by the various magical tests, a quick confession is extorted from her by torture. She is then summarily disposed of.

All Christian missionaries admit that these beliefs constitute the greatest obstacle to genuine conversion. Whatever else has changed on the continent of Africa, the deep-rooted belief in magic both white and black, has not. And no one can say how many innocent men and women have been terrified, tortured and even murdered as a result of the African's obsession with witchcraft.

HAUNTED

There are many places in the continent that have known tragedy and human hurt and have become dwelling places of demons. Just as evil spirits are territorial, so are wizards and witches. The more evil the spirits, the stronger the demons that control the wizards and witches, the more important and larger the territory the possessed person will control. For instance, one witch could control a river while a wizard could control a city or nation.

The Bible says that "...we wrestle not against flesh and blood... but against spiritual wickedness in high places" (Ephesians 6:12). There are principalities of demon authority. A principality is an area where a prince rules his subjects. This means that in the world of evil spirits there are categories of authority and areas which certain spirits rule.

There are evil spirits which command other spirits. They will fight each other over the possession of a body. The use of witchcraft is a deliberate and intentional interaction with the devil or familiar spirit using unearthly powers of evil to accomplish Satan's plans to materialize upon the earth.

There is no love or good among demons. They are full of division and cause humans to be in a like manner Praise God for mercy! Jesus extended His grace to me and gave me life and canceled my eternal death sentence. The Bible says in the Old Testament, "Thou shalt not suffer a witch to live" (Exodus 22:18). In the New Testament first Jesus Christ Himself and then the power of His name and the blood sacrifice alone can recover a witch or wizard from the clutches of Satan.

Interest in the occult is idolatry and is a clear violation of the First Commandment (Exodus 20:3–5). The Bible warns that idolatry is "fellowship with devils" and provokes "the Lord to jealousy" (1 Corinthians 10:20-22).

Seeking help from the occult is the same as calling upon another god. It is insulting to God who made heaven and earth to consult with a demon inspired person for spiritual guidance and to participate is an abomination before God and will bring His swift judgment upon the person involved, also their descendants. "Thou shalt have no other gods before me. Thou shalt not bow down thyself unto them, nor serve them: for I the Lord thy God am a jealous God, visiting the iniquity of the fathers upon the children unto the third and fourth generation of them that hate me" (Deuteronomy 5: 7, 9).

There are many Christian churches in Africa that are like those in the United States and Europe. Missionaries took Christianity to Africa. Also we have numerous Africans that are Muslims because the Arabs couldn't see a Muslim as a slave, so many Africans converted to escape slavery. Even though many Africans practice Christianity and Islam, multitudes still pray to their ancestor's spirits for strength, advice, and wisdom. This is exactly where I fit into God's spiritual strategy for Africa. As a former witch doctor, Jesus called me out of the darkness from a fourth-generational witch doctor family to expose the powers of darkness. My family enjoyed an elite position, was known in the city of Cape Coast, and known as powerful witch doctors. We were feared because our ruthless reputation of evil that had reached into the highest places.

POWER OF JESUS

I have good news for you. Jesus Christ is busy bringing to His Church the full truth of Satan's total defeat. After my born again experience, Jesus appeared to me and said, "Vagalas, I am calling you into my church because my people are blinded to the working of demons. I am sending you to teach my church about deliverance to cleanse My Church to set them free."

Since Jesus has brought me into this ministry of miracles and deliverance, I have met many other deliverance ministers around the world that he has called and trained for such a time as this. He calls them the "hidden ones." He says that He will suddenly start bringing these other powerful ministers to the forefront. He will cleanse His Church and have a Bride without spot or wrinkle.

Our God is faithful. He is moving in a great revival in Ghana. A spiritual revolution is shaking the continent of Africa. We feel the breezes of His mighty wind blowing across the land into the faces of a people, who are eager for spiritual freedom and are ready for His light, "Here am I; send me!"

Praise His Name!

PART 2:

FOURTH GENERATION WITCH DOCTOR FINDS JESUS

Chapter One

Witch Doctor—Yes to Jesus

It is the work of God by which each one of us, as a hell-deserving sinner, can receive a new life. It is a second birth, a spiritual birth.*

NEW CREATURE

Think about this. I am a new creation in Christ Jesus! I have a new bloodline. I am a new breed, a new creation! The Bible says that a new creation is a being that exists that never existed before. God has regenerated my spirit making me completely new! According to the Word, "Because the creature itself also shall be delivered from the bondage of corruption into the glorious liberty of the children of God" (Romans 8:21).

THE WITCH DOCTOR AND JESUS

In those days, a person could not come up to me and say, "Jesus loves you." No one would dare to do such a thing. Everybody knew me in Africa. I was so powerful, so wicked, and so strong. After salvation, it took about six months before I had a human heart because my heart was so demonized. So I could not feel anything. My conversion to Jesus was really a supernatural sovereign act of God.

It was a hot scorching Saturday night. I was trying to sleep. The moon was shining through the window at its highest point. I was restless. My eyes felt like I had toothpicks holding them open. As I gazed at the shadows in the room, thousands of thoughts ran through

---

* Adapted from Paul J. Levin, *The New Birth* (Bloomington, IL: Bible Tracts, 2000).

my mind. I could not get my brain to shut down. My body was tense, but I closed my eyes.

No one had ever told me about Jesus. I was suddenly awakened and I heard a voice call my name, "Vagalas, Vagalas, Kanco, Kanco, get up." I opened my eyes and looked around the room. It was about four-thirty or five o'clock. Looking around, I didn't see anyone. So I was trying to contact the demon that was speaking but I couldn't see him. Whenever a wizard serves Satan, he's only allowed to sleep for about two hours. He demands his agent to work like a machine. The devils can easily control a wizard when he is weak and tired.

"Vagalas," a strange voice spoke my name. As soon as I heard my name, I got up and tried to contact the spirits. I wanted to tell them that today I didn't have anything to do. So when I contacted the spirit from the east, he wasn't there. Then I contacted the demons from the west, south and north. This was very unusual and I began to wonder why? In fact, this had never happened before. Consequently, I tried to contact them again. Still, they were not available.

Accordingly, I left my body with my spirit and flew to the second chamber. I tried to find the demon that was directly in charge of me. Funny, he was gone too! When I came back and my spirit entered back into my body, I felt drained. I fell asleep. Between five thirty and six o'clock, the same spiritual voice spoke, "Vagalas, Vagalas, get up." I was stunned because this was a strange voice that I had never heard before. Looking around the room, I could not see this Spirit's presence. It seemed empty. This was very bizarre because the demons were not visible. In the past, they were always there, watching and guarding me.

"Vagalas," the voice spoke firmly. I rubbed my eyes and shook my head.

"Vagalas, get up. Go take a bath." I sat up. This is a strange command, I thought. Wizards don't take baths. Every demon knows this fact. Usually, they are allowed by the spirits to go once a year to bathe in rivers. Besides the demons would only let me sleep about fifteen minutes at a time. They are tormentors who love to put me in misery and keep me weak. What's going on? Out of the blue, panic raced through my mind.

I replied to the invisible voice, "You know that with my kind of work, I don't have to shower."

Ignoring my response, the voice repeated, "Vagalas, go take a bath."

So I decided to contact the spirits from the north, east, south and west again. Nothing! All this time, I felt that something was wrong. This situation was odd. In spite of everything, it didn't seem right. But in Satan's kingdom, I dared not to rebel. I knew that I had to obey the spirits' orders before complaining. If I had any disagreements, I knew it was important for me to do the work first. Whenever I returned to see the demons, they would command me to "sit down." Demons believe that people are inferior to themselves. Besides, they hate them. However, they are legalists and if I could prove my case, they'd listen to me.

Regardless of the snare that Satan sets for a person, you can be sure of one thing it will be fun in the beginning but their fun will turn into a nightmare before their eyes. Any covenant that is entered into with evil spirits has been documented under the sea. It's there! They don't just joke. In fact, if a person has ever gone to a witch doctor or a soothsayer, whatever was said, it's there. It has been written and it will be used against them and their children. It is written!

Most of the time, I felt like a puppet that was being controlled by powerful strong demons. They always did whatever they wanted to me. They had deceived me to the point that I thought that I was controlling them! Thinking back now, I knew that I was truly a slave to the powers of darkness.

"Vagalas," the strange voice said, "get up and bathe." Although I didn't recognize the voice, I slavishly obeyed.

The sunlight came up and streams of light were coming through the cracks in the curtains. I rubbed my eyes because I did not like the daytime.

After the bath, the voice continued, "Today we are going to the Assembly of God."

I replied to the invisible spirit, "But we don't do these things in the daytime. We do our work at night." Then before another second, a big invisible hand grabbed me by my pant's belt in the back and began to push me out the room. The hand took me across the street to an Assembly of God church.

Shocked, I struggled, pushing my body back, I sternly said, "I can't go in there. We don't go in churches during the daytime. We only strike in these places spiritually at night." The hand was there and I was being pushed forward, walking and walking. The hand just continued to push me forward, thrusting me into the church.

I could hear the demons hooting, moaning and screaming, "Oh shame, shame. ACK, shame, shame." They shrieked and covered their faces with their hands and some had their hands over their ears.

It was strange. My hands were trembling and then my arms began to shake. What was happening was I could not keep myself still. The demons began to shriek in my head and blaspheme the church and Jesus Christ, cursing those rebellious people.

It was like an unusual spiritual force that hit me in the face when I slipped through the door. I wanted to turn and run away but I could not because the invisible hand had a firm hold on me. I felt a strange atmosphere in the building. I had never felt anything like it in my life. Finally, the invisible hand pushed me down in the last pew of the church.

I was amazed because these people had always been considered my enemies. Why did the spirits bring me into this place, I wondered? They hated churches and used us to infiltrate and tear these churches apart. In fact, we never went into these places in the daytime. Later I discovered that I was there by a divine appointment of God.

They were singing and praising God with joy. Their songs were piercing through my cold heart, "Jesus, Jesus, Jesus, there's just something about that Name." The music was causing a great turmoil in my spirit. My mouth was dry. I was miserable but sat silently.

As the service continued the atmosphere became even more charged emotionally. I had a strange experience when the people raised their voices in worship.

My body was trembling. Fear was shouting in my mind, "Get out of here, now!"

There were hymns also; "Amazing Grace," "All Hail the Power of Jesus' Name," "Alleluia—Alleluia." The people stood with their eyes closed, hands lifted, their bodies swaying, singing in deep worship to Jesus Christ. However, some, in terror were turning and looking at me. I had never seen anything like it in my entire life.

A demonic voice inside of me kept saying, "Get out of here. You belong to me." The tone of the voice sent shivers up and down my spine. Another voice was saying, "Just follow Me, I will save you."

Then the preacher saw me. He had the most shocked expression on his face that I had ever seen. He stopped the music and looked right at me. He began to extend his hands toward my direction. His eyes were opened wide, he said, "Any spirit who thinks he is so powerful and he has come here to disturb our meeting, we come against that person in the name of Jesus."

I chuckled to myself. They know me so they didn't believe that I would come there to worship their God.

When he saw me there, he thought I was there to play evil tricks. So he said, "Anybody who is here to play tricks with God, he will see God is more powerful. I bind you in the name of Jesus." He was praying against me. He was insulting me. His voice was loud—very nervous.

Everyone in town knew me. They were fully aware that members of my family were powerful key witch doctors in the area.

"Anyone who is here to bring devils into this church is bound in the name of Jesus," the pastor said, wildly waving his hands toward the sky.

A cold sweat broke out over my entire body. My mouth felt like a cotton ball; my throat tight, scorched as I stiffened my body. My hands became very clammy. Looking around, I noticed that I could not move a muscle in fear, but I could feel the serpentine spirit moving up and down my spine. Yes that is exactly what I felt. Stark fear. If the preacher only knew what was happening inside of me, they would have had pity for me.

He said, "Let's pray for anybody who may have evil ideas. Let's pray against any demons." For two hours, while they were praying to bind the demons, my spirit and body were being tormented. They were destroying my strongholds and there was a great struggle for my soul.

An explosion of demonic voices was groaning and whining. They sounded like a chorus moaning from a horror movie and screaming inside of my head as well as the outside as they continued hooting.

The air was infused with shouts as the demons roared, "Get out of here. Don't listen to those rebellious people," the demons hissed like snakes (demons referred to Christians as "those rebellious people").

My fingernails tightly clenched were digging a ridge into the palms of my hands. "We hate them," the demons growled. "Remember how much you hate them too."

It was then that I realized that these powers were truly controlling me and I was not, as I had thought, controlling them! The demons were angry and wanted me to charge out but they could not move me because Christ's power is stronger. The invisible hand held me tightly in the pew.

The people were dismayed. They were very much scared because the preacher's voice was high pitched and screaming loudly, "Jesus, Jesus, I bind every evil spirit in your name." His body was moving like a karate warrior.

There was a strange physical energy or intensity surrounding me. I found myself shaking and trembling. I was nauseated and feeling very weak.

Then he preached from the book of Daniel, "There was a king. He wanted to destroy God."

The people shouted, "Preach on."

"God turned him into a beast."

"Preach!" The people shouted and then they would turn and look at me and say, "Amen."

The air was charged with spiritual authority. The preacher gave a call for spiritual healing. He said, "If you have never received Jesus Christ as your Savior, this call is for you." I felt an intensity building in me and could hear my heart beating. "If you repent from your sins, ask Him to forgive you, He will receive you into His kingdom. The Apostle Peter said, "Repent and be baptized every one of you in the name of Jesus Christ for the remission of your sins and you shall receive the Holy Ghost" (Acts 2:38).

I wanted to put my hands over my ears run out the door. However, the invisible hand was holding me in place and I could not move. The words were cutting into my heart.

I had tormenting spirits inside of me and I could hear them groaning and wailing, "Get out of here Get out of here. These people are crazy, leave, leave." It was during this great struggle that I realized that these spirits were controlling me. Really, these spirits were not under my control because they were being subjected to a stronger power. I wanted to leave, but the invisible hand had me anchored in the seat. This was a true supernatural confrontation with the forces of good and evil—Jesus and the Devil. Something was piercing though my dark mind.

Then suddenly I felt the hand lifting me up. I began moving toward the front of the church. Every eye in the place watched in fear.

When I was coming, the preacher said, "Hold it—hold it. Do you know what you are doing?"

"Yes."

"Are you sure that you understand what you are doing? You are coming for Jesus?" He seemed nervous. "I come against you with the blood of Jesus. Demons can't stand in the presence of the blood of Jesus."

When you hold the blood of Jesus before a demon, you are simply reminding him of his defeat. The devil knows he is defeated but you are merely telling him that you know it too.

"Are you sure that you know what you are doing?"

I just stood there looking at him.

The preacher was really prepared for battle now. "I bind you—you have no power here. I come against you with the blood of Jesus." He was rapidly moving back and forth like a cat. "I soak myself in the Blood of Jesus." He was poised for spiritual war

I continued to stand there shuddering, staring at him as I was taller than he was. In fact, I towered over him (I am a very tall African of six-feet-six). He was still trying to size up the situation. There was something highly unusual happening here and he knew it. He was bold and with his teeth clenched he said, "Do you want to receive Jesus?"

I felt the invisible hand tighten around my belt. "Yes. I do want to receive Jesus."

Shocked, he said to the congregation, "Pray, pray, pray." He continued, "Will you repent from your sin, you know, err—your idolatry, witchcraft?"

"Yes," I replied. It was then that I noticed that tears were surging down my cheeks. Something was happening inside me that had never happened to me before. I had never cried in my life. African men don't cry. Besides, I was hard and had a demonized heart. I was cold, angry, full of hate. I didn't quite understand what was happening, but it was something that was not natural. It was grabbing my entire body with raw emotion. My mind felt dizzy.

The voices of the demons were muffled and I heard a different voice. I received the Lord Jesus. It was gentle. "Welcome, my son."

The preacher was overcome by emotion and had wrapped his arms around my neck. He was gushing unintelligent words and weeping. "My God, praise You, Jesus." I felt an odd sensation. No one had ever hugged me like that before, including my father or mother.

When I received the Lord, I thought that the hand would leave me, but it didn't. It tightly held me again. Then I felt the hand moving me down the aisle and out the door. The invisible hand took me back to my bed and pushed me into it. I fell into a deep sleep and slept for the first time since I could remember, from about one o'clock until twelve-thirty at night. (Satan would never let me sleep more than two hours each night).

Chapter Two

The Man Appears

Several nights later, I saw a strange man appear at the foot of my bed and light flooded the room. My heart began to flutter and I tell you, I experienced great fear. This Man was awesome. He was surrounded by light. His eyes flashed with fire. He had a crown of thorns around His head and blood was seeping out. He held his hands toward me. They were pierced and had blood flowing from them.

I felt the greatest love and compassion pouring from His eyes. After a few minutes, He disappeared. He did not speak.

I ran to my pastor. "Pastor, I am very frightened. I saw a man. He came to me with a crown of thorns upon His head and there was blood flowing from His hands."

Isn't it funny? I was never afraid of demonic spirits but Jesus' appearance is fearful and awesome. I told him about the appearance.

"What did He say?" The pastor asked.

"Nothing," I replied.

"If He appears again," the pastor said, "Listen to what He has to say and come tell me."

The second night, the man appeared again. "He didn't say a thing," I told the pastor again. He prayed for me.

The third night, He appeared again. I opened my eyes and sat up in my bed. I saw Jesus standing at the foot of my bed. He was standing in a bright light. His white robe was tied with a golden sash that loosely hung to His feet. His eyes glowed like fiery coals. Yet, I could see compassion in them.

His fierce presence inspired an awesome fear in me. He pointed his finger toward me and I could see He had scarred hands. The imprints were still there. Every cell in my body was alive to His presence. I was trembling and tears were trickling down my cheeks.

This time He spoke and said, "Vagalas, I am Jesus." I was drawn to his eyes. They were filled with peace and love. "I have called you into My Church. I delivered you out of great darkness to go and tell My people what I have done for you. Tell them that I came to die for them and to rescue them from these evil spirits. All your sins have been forgiven. I want you to tell My Church that my power is greater."

I felt absolute peace because He was not an invisible spiritual being. I could see Him!

Then He said, "Teach them about the reality of demons and my power to overcome the darkness because My Church does not understand the darkness that they are facing. I love you. Fear not, for I will be with you all the days of your life. And they will understand what you have done and see everything I have done for you. Tell them about these things because I am coming soon—I am coming soon—I am coming soon," His voice seemed to fade.

His voice sounded like rushing waters, an echo. His words pierced my soul down to the very bone. Then, He suddenly vanished.

I rushed back to my pastor and told him, "the Man has spoken."

I was very scared. "Can I sleep here between you and your wife?" I begged.

He prayed with me. I was shaking with a great fear. He prayed about so many things. He prayed for about six hours.

FAMILY FEAR

Praise God, I got saved before my father was able to transfer his spiritual powers to me! However, he was training me to become his successor. After I received Jesus, it caused a great spiritual chaos within my immediate family. Within ten days my uncle came to me and told me that if I did not return to them, the demons had threatened to kill members of my family. The demons said that I had broken the ranks in the spiritual realms with the Devil. The challenge went out that threatened the lives of my mother, her sons, and my father's brothers.

My mother was angered by my "rebellion." Her mouth tightened in a line. She sat like that for a few seconds and then she said, "no!" She slammed her hand on the table. She felt new spiritual winds blowing against her entire lifestyle. I did not blame her for her rage because she was defending the only god that she knew. She had spent her whole life serving these gods. She felt they had been good to her by giving her sons. She had also been the assistant to my father in his witchcraft. Tears were running down her face. She pleaded with me to serve her gods, "Look at what you are giving up. You are chosen to take over the power of your father as the first born." I could see the terror in her eyes, the flush of her face, the trembling of her hands, as she was very animated in making her points

I forgave her, because she was only trying to protect me and had fear of the demons killing her sons. She wept, cried, screamed and threatened me and begged me to return to my family's honor. She threatened never to speak to me again as long as I live. Then she stalked out of my room, weeping uncontrollably.

Satan took this opportunity to whisper in my head, "Just open the door once more and I'll never let you go."

A thought popped into my head. It was something that my pastor had said, "Reject the devil's lies and live. Swallow them and burn forever!"

The day came for a show down and Jesus' power was proven. In the end, I didn't return to the kingdom of Satan. I stood firmly in my commitment to Jesus Christ.

Then the remaining members of my family began to give their lives to Jesus. The Lord was faithful to his Word as shown in (Acts 2: 38–39), "Then Peter said unto them, Repent, and be baptized every one of you in the name of Jesus Christ for the remission of sins, and ye shall receive the gift of the Holy Ghost. For the promise is unto you, and to your children, and to all that are afar off, even as many as the Lord our God shall call." Jesus was true to His Word, even saving several of my uncles. They saw the power of Jesus operating in my life. I totally wanted to give my life to the Lord because I felt His protection and love for me. The blessings of Abraham are now following me instead of the curses of the devils. Death came to the family of the uncle who had threatened me and not to my family.

THE GENERAL OVERSEER OF THE ASSEMBLY OF GOD

Later, my pastor took me to the General Overseer of the Assembly of God of Ghana. The preacher told the overseer that I had been through fear and terror and this and that—but this is what I was saying. I told them about last night's visitations and what the Man had told me. He told me that my sins were forgiven. That He was calling me to stand in the church and preach, telling His people what I had done.

The overseer asked, "What have you done?"

"I have done a lot. I have done many evil things."

He said, "Tell me."

I started telling him. The overseer fainted on the floor. He had never heard anything like it before. At this time, it was so new, that the man just collapsed. Later, he encouraged me and told me to wait and Jesus would show me what to do.

SPIRITUAL BATTLES

I went through many spiritual battles to break free of the Devil's clutches. Some Christians are afraid to face the reality of demons and satanic activities. It's overwhelming to them, but we don't have to live in fear. We must know our authority in Christ and pray and intercede for them and to love those who oppose us.

We are in a war to reclaim what the Devil stole. The Bible tells us that we defeat him through the blood of Jesus. We must be faithful to stand in the authority of Jesus knowing that Jesus can bring down the kingdom of Satan. We must conquer the land—to cast out devils. This requires aggressiveness against the enemy over whom we have been given great authority.

Leaving witchcraft behind required a total life change. I went through two years of deliverance. It was another two years before I was allowed to speak in the churches concerning my life. In Africa, the Assembly of God Churches will not allow people to stand in their pulpits just because they have a strong experience with the Lord. They watch to see if you are real. Then you must go to Bible school and then you can speak from the pulpits. After ministering on the streets, telling people about Jesus and casting demons out of the possessed people, then the pastors began to take me in.

"Let's protect him," they said. "He appears to be real. He is still standing for Christ."

Jesus Christ's power prevailed in my life and today; I am a born-again Christian, washed in His holy blood, free!

The Bible says, "But if I cast out devils by the Spirit of God, then the kingdom of God is come unto you" (Matthew 12:28).

I truly believe that Jesus is the only answer for Africa. When I stepped out of the darkness, there was the most beautiful clear light. My life will be spent telling my people the truth of whom Jesus Christ truly is. He is the Savior of our souls.

THE VALUE OF FAITH

The Christian faith is unique, not because it recognizes man's problems and needs, but because it also recognizes that man cannot do anything by himself to solve his problems or meet his needs. Only Jesus can save and deliver a person from the powers of darkness.

It's true. Everybody needs Christ! The Bible tells us, "Ye shall know the truth and the truth shall make you free" (John 8:32).

Jesus pleads invitingly. "I am the way, the truth, and the life: no man cometh unto the Father, but by me" (John 14:6). "Verily, verily I am the door of the sheep" (John 10:7). "Neither is there salvation in any other: for there is none other name under heaven given among men, whereby we must be saved" (Acts 4:12).

I know that every soul born on this earth is lost at birth because they come into this world under the sin of Adam and Eve, our first parents. Adam submitted his will to the devil, sinned and therefore, lost eternal life for all mankind. His lost condition may be described as falling short of the glory of God. Adam was trapped in a difficult situation, apart from God, filled with regret, in a world he never made. He brought corruption, disease and poverty into that world. That bondage of sin and its consequence creates an alienation from one's fellow man and God. Men's own unaided efforts to solve their problems through intellectual, economic, political, social or psychological skills are destined to fail.

I was taught in Bible school that salvation is a free gift from God. It is a work of God in which He rescues man from eternal ruin. Thank God that he saw in darkness. He had mercy on my soul. Glory to God! The doom of sin granted to me the riches of His grace, even eternal life beginning now and eternal glories in heaven forevermore. From the moment you are saved, if you will let God do it in your spirit, you will begin to enjoy the fruits of salvation. In fact, salvation of God is for those who do not deserve it and have no preparation for it.

Do you know what is a true believer according to the Bible shown in Hebrews 10:32–39? Are you a true believer? Believers look only to the Bible for eternal answers. The Bible alone can give correct and complete answers to our spiritual questions. Look to the days after salvation when there came many afflictions, (verse 32), when you were made a gazing stock and as were your companions (33) you supported the ministry, (34), do not cast away his confidence, (35), exercise patience, (36), do the will of God and receive the promises, (36), look for the coming of Jesus, (37), the just shall live by faith (38), believe the saving of the soul and do not draw back into the abode of Satan and the forces of evil, where sinners suffer eternal punishment. Actually when you are born again, your spirit inside of you becomes alive.

Before Christ walks into your life, your spirit inside of you is dead to God. You don't know God. You have no communication with Him. Therefore, you are cut off from God and that means spiritual death. Look at Romans 5:12: "Wherefore, as by one man sin entered into the world, and death by sin; and so death passed upon all men, for that all have sinned."

SPIRITUAL FRUIT

Upon salvation, a person is saved spiritually and physically at the resurrection for eternity. However, to claim His name without the new life is a fatal deception!

Jesus lovingly cautions, "Not everyone that saith unto me, Lord, Lord, shall enter into the kingdom of heaven; but he that doeth the will of my Father which is in heaven." (Matthew 7:21–23). It is certainly true that Jesus said, "I am the vine, ye are the branches . . . If a man abide not in me, he is cast forth as a branch and is withered: and men gather them, and cast them into the fire and they are burned." (John 15:5,6).

Romans chapter 8, which was written for Christians, lists 34 blessings for saints. Saints are born again Christians. It solemnly warns against an empty profession and offers glorious assurance for those who abide in Christ, and bear fruit. "For if ye live after the flesh, ye shall die: but if ye through the Spirit do mortify the deeds of the body, ye shall live" (Romans 8:13).

If you are born again, you are a new creature in Christ! 2 Corinthians 5:17 says: "Therefore if any man be in Christ, he is a new creature: old things are passed away; behold all things are become new." The new birth is a spiritual regeneration (2 Peter 1:4; 1 Peter 1:23), spiritual quickening or resurrection (Ephesians 2:2,5,6). In regeneration you are quickened out of your spiritual estrangement and isolation from God you are supernaturally transferred into a spiritual life of union and communion with God.

Your resurrection is the restoration to life of that which the old life has become extinct. The Bible says, "For then must he often have suffered since the foundation of the world: but now once in the end of the world hath he appeared to put alway sin by the sacrifice of himself" (Hebrews 9:26).

It is a spiritual transformation according to Colossians 1:13. Regeneration is a transfer out of one kingdom to another. It's a transfer out of the kingdom of darkness in which sin and Satan rules into the kingdom of God's dear Son.

The problem of slavery to sin is that it is an alien concept in a modern world. For instance, it relies upon the studies of human nature and upon psychoanalysis, self-improvement, self-esteem, human potential, New Age thinking and other self-help psychologies and philosophies.

These popular theories rob the modern world of any rhyme or reason for thinking about sin. The contention is that people are basically good; let's try to make them even better. Is it any wonder, then, that some people today place the reality of sin alongside that of the existence of UFOs? This seems incredible, but just few misguided souls. However, when you know your true human condition you are not easily deceived, you know differently. You also know that there is no possibility of remedial self-help from what the Bible calls sin. It is a disheartening situation, really. You feel the strength of sin within and wish that you could be "saved" from it, but at the same time you recognize yourself as utterly powerless to change situations.

The solution is redemption. It's a spiritual creation, "In whom we have redemption through his blood, the forgiveness of sins, according to the riches of his grace" (Ephesians 1:7). The apostle Paul goes on to write in Ephesians 2:13: "But now in Christ Jesus ye who sometimes were far off are made nigh by the blood of Christ."

Jesus is the Creator (John 1:3). He is the only Savior (Acts 4:12). He will be the Judge (John 5:22, 27; Acts 10:42). Christ is our blessing! "Let the Lord be magnified, which hath pleasure in the prosperity of his servant" (Psalms 35:27).

Chapter Three

The Truth Shall Make You Free

The Spirit of the Lord is upon me, because he hath anointed me to preach the gospel to the poor; he hath sent me to heal the brokenhearted, to preach deliverance to the captives, and recovering of sight to the blind, to set at liberty them that are bruised. (Luke 4:18)

FREEDOM

Everybody needs Christ and everybody needs deliverance! "Ye shall know the truth and the truth shall make you free" (John 8:32). Every soul born on this earth is lost at birth because they come into this world under the sin of Adam and Eve, our first parents. Adam submitted his will to the devil, sinned and therefore lost eternal life for all mankind. His lost condition may be described as falling short of the glory of God.

Jesus asserts, "I am the way, the truth, and the life; no man cometh to the Father, but by me" (John 14:6). When I got saved, the demons alerted the powers in the city under the sea. Of course I had fear. I had worked with these demons many years. I had witnessed their power, their evil hate, and their murderous natures. Each time the hindering devils came to ensnare me Jesus always gave me a way of escape.

It took a lot of love, prayer and fasting to set me totally free. Thank God for giving me a pastor who gave the time that I needed. He guided me through those terrible times of rejection and spiritual oppression. The devil doesn't like to lose even one of his captives. He fights to keep every soul. He uses demons, unsaved people and some Christians to do things to discourage them.

There were terrible rejections because they were afraid of me. Many Christians turned against me and begin to criticize, gossip, murmur, and grumble and oppose me. I needed someone who would stand by my side and stand against the evil and false charges that were being hurled at me. I became confused in my heart and frustrated. My new pastor stood with me. I did not know the Bible but I tried to read it anyway. I could not understand it but I knew that Jesus was real and that He had called me to "go and testify what I have done for you."

The turmoil hung around me like a very dark cloud. Only a close walk with Jesus Christ brought me though this hostile and lonely time. I was like a person between two worlds. In the beginning, both were combative to me. I made it because my wise pastor nurtured me with the Word of God and his love. And then, Jesus stayed very close to me. I could hear His gentle words of encouragement and feel Him bathing me with his love. He was preparing me to bring me safely into God's Kingdom. There is the assurance of God's eternal deliverance—of being rescued from death and transported into the Lord's heavenly kingdom!

Only Christians possess authority from Jesus to cast out evil spirits. Too often Christians and others are prone to be skeptical about the existence of spirits and demons. But they do exist and they are responsible to Satan for deceiving curious humans. "And every spirit that confesseth not that Jesus Christ is come in the flesh is not of God: and this is that spirit of Antichrist, whereof ye have heard that it should come; and even now already is it in the world" (1 John 4:3).

THE BATTLE IS THE LORD'S

I was no stranger to demons. I had called upon them and they came to my aid I thought I controlled them but actually they had control of me! Now I could see that they were my enemies. Since I turned against them and had joined the army of Jesus Christ they have tried everything they could think of to kill me. I know the reality of their violent powers. The demons tormented me and threatened. I felt there was someone in my head but could not understand what they were saying. My head would begin to throb, the pain pounding against my eyeballs like a hammer. Jesus would minister to me and the fear and oppression would lift. Many times, the demons would follow me and hassle me in my mind. They told me that they would never give me peace. Jesus showed me that I needed deliverance.

He told me, "Do not be afraid. I love you and I have proved it by dying on the cross and paying the penalty for your sins. Trust Me My child because I have demonstrated My power by rising from the grave."

Being a newborn baby Christian, I had to learn to live in a new supernatural world, and to change my allegiance from my former connections with the powers of darkness. As a new Christian I am now a sworn enemy of the legions of hell and like all people, whoever they were before they became Christians, I was in sin. Some were idolaters, some were adulterous, some horoscope readers, witches or warlocks, and some fornicators. They must not have any delusions about Satan's reality or their hostility to God.

Jesus told me that I must not fear or believe the devils. The Lord showed me that the devils do not have any power over me and that the Lord Jesus inside of me terrifies the devils.

"The devils cannot touch you, but they will try to seduce you," Jesus warned.

I remember that when I was practicing witchcraft, if a person became a serious Christian, the devils would target him. I knew that I was in for a knock-down battle with the forces of evil. Every Christian at times will experience great opposition. My pastor taught me to call upon the name of Jesus and ask the Lord to send warring angels to protect me. He said to read the Bible and always lean upon the Lord.

SATAN'S DISADVANTAGE

As I grew in the Lord, I found that the Bible reveals that the devil is at a great disadvantage concerning his power over Christians. He is shown as an inferior adversary in light of the power that Jesus Christ gave to His Church. Satan can only take the place that he is given. The Word of God says "Submit yourselves therefore to God. Resist the devil and he will flee from you" (James 4:7).

The Scripture makes it very clear to me that the battle is not my personal battle. Though I am a part of the war, the battle is the Lord's.

The unconquerable One leads us. The battle rests upon His ability and He has already won the war!

Thank God that I learned that Jesus Christ is the only mediator between God and man (1 Timothy 2:5). His mission was fully accomplished. He is in full control and is exalted to the Father's right hand. He is the Master with almighty power. Jesus came to defy the power of Satan (Acts 26:18). He challenged the rule of Satan (Colossians 2:10) and conquered the right to dominion (Colossians 2:14,15). He set us free from the penalty for sin (1 Peter 3:18). He can set us free from the curse of sin (1 Peter 5:10).

Chapter Four

Triumph Over Evil

And ye shall know the truth, and the truth shall make you free. (John 8:32)

HIGHWAY TO LIBERTY

I have found that life with Jesus Christ is exciting and blessed with constant triumph over evil forces, but the battle never ends. I always remember that with Jesus, I am in the majority. The warfare is stacked against Satan, not the Christian. It is true that I have had periods of darkness and encountered times of painful struggle and discouragement. However, when the Holy Spirit broke through the darkness, moments of exultation and the glory of God were experienced. God is always on my side!

In the beginning, Jesus supernaturally delivered me from many tormenting devils. Then He used some ministers to help free me from the powers of darkness. The deliverance ministry was not really practiced much in Africa when I first got saved. People actually would faint when I tried to tell them about my witchcraft experiences. I really had to depend on Jesus and my pastors.

My deliverance didn't take ten minutes or ten days, but more than two long years before I was delivered from manipulating, unclean, tormenting and lying witchcraft spirits. Blood washed pastors who knew the power of the blood of Jesus Christ over all demons eagerly ministered to me. After they were truly convinced that I had made a full commitment to Christ and was willing to establish him as Lord of my life, they began to remove the demons of the powers of darkness from my life. The Bible says that if an evil spirit is cast out, he goes to the dry places. He finds no peace, so he returns and if he does not find that person filled with the things of God he will bring seven worse devils back with him.

Believe me, when one comes from the depth of evil that I did complete deliverance just doesn't happen in a day. My pastor loved me and committed to stand with me until the bitter end. Many pastors came together and challenged and made war with the forces of evil that were inside of me. They had to deal with and defeat the powers and principalities that were struggling to hold on to me from the outside. It wasn't easy to get free. I had to keep my will in agreement with the Word and stand against the devils that were trying to hold on to me. It was a fierce struggle and there were times when I wondered if I could make it. However, Jesus was always working with me. In the darkest moments I could feel Him encouraging me not to quit. Since I could see into the spiritual realms it made me determined not to give up.

From the beginning of my conversion, Satan's agents started chasing me. They tormented me in my dreams. They commanded me to come back. They challenged my new life and told me that they would never leave me to enjoy any peace until I return to the City Under the Sea. They told me that I was a marked man—marked for death. Satan told them himself to make me their number one target.

"You can run to the ends of the world, but you will never be able to hide," they screamed into my ears. The hindrances and harassing devils were always there—grinning, shouting obscenities and threatening their vengeance upon me. I saw them everywhere. The deeper one goes into the powers of darkness, the greater the bondage!

I was scared, no doubt about it. The bedeviling spirits meant business. Without Jesus, I could not have made it, that's for sure. However, I had seen Jesus and I knew His glory and power. I trusted Him and He gave the faith and strength that I needed to get through these horrendous times. Before deliverance on occasions I experienced periods of blackouts. I was plagued by nightmares and tormented in my mind. There was a great warfare going on for control of my body, but Jesus would be the Victor. My insides began to quiver the way they had when I was a boy during my initiation rites. Throughout my deliverance sometimes I was unconscious of what was happening.

At other times, I was fully aware of the fierce battle that was raging inside and outside of me.

The pastors' prayers were penetrating the veil between the worlds. There was a fierce spiritual warfare going on. The angelic host of God and the foul demons of hell were engaging in a battle for my body. I could feel my stomach tighten with apprehension and hear the demons groaning and gnashing their teeth. I saw many of them in their demonic forms leaving me. Some were like monsters. Some were shaped like animals while others were like sea creatures. Spirits came out that looked like sea serpents, crocodiles, octopuses, crabs, whales, fish, sharks, squids, and mermaids. Some looked like snakes, monkeys, chickens, pigs, evil ferocious monsters and beasts. There were legions of them. Their faces were gnarly and twisted with fear. There were many big, black giants hovering in the room. A whispered scream forced itself through my lips, twisting the muscles of my mouth like a distasteful medicine.

I could also see the angelic hosts of God. There was a strategic warfare going on between these demons and the angelic hosts. I saw armies of warrior angels. They looked like men with incredible physiques and shining beauty. Some appeared in their angelic forms with wings. The demons seemed to be in great fear of these angels. They were battling grotesque creatures with reptilian faces and thousands of disfigured forms. It was a hand-to-hand combat. They were fighting the demons with flaming swords that were twisting and flashing. However, the most interesting thing that I was witnessing was that both armies were responding to the words being spoken by God's ministers!

"We hate you," they screamed. The demons also seemed to fear the ministers. They seemed to fight to hold onto my body because whenever a demon was cast out, an angel quickly bound and captured him and took him away.

The demons were screeching in loud voices "Have you come to destroy us before our time? Leave us alone! His mother promised him. He belongs to us. He was promised to us by his father."

The deliverance ministers just seemed to ignore everything that they were doing and saying and continued to press them to leave. It felt as though a million demons were slapping and kicking me. Some people would hold my feet and others were restraining my arms. I could feel my facial expression change when suddenly the demonic spirits took over my personality. Sometimes my face felt as though the skin was being ripped off. The ungodly creature would take control of my eyes and glance around the room. I heard him say that he was looking to see if there was a hypocrite in the room. "I must obey his commands but I will go to another body," he said. A shudder dislodged every bit of my composure. Again I heard his voice repeating that he wanted to find another body to enter but could not see one. "Aaaaa-ah" I cried, my voice strangely distorted my body arching upward. My stomach felt as if a million razor blades were slashing me, bending me forward in excruciating pain.

The pastor spoke, "I bind the strongman. You have no power here. I bind your power over Vagalas' mind, body or spirit. You must leave in Jesus' name."

A spiritually shaped giant octopus spirit held me tightly, gripping my chest with all its strength. It was trying to take my breath away. His legs were deeply embedded in various parts of my body. The evil thing growled, and I found myself shaking, trembling, and withering and weeping like a defeated child. Then I thrashed around like a fish. These were marine spirits. They were very powerfully rooted in my life because of the time that I spent in the evil City Under the Sea

All present could see manifestations of the demons and begin to pray for God's protection and the Blood of Jesus. Someone was singing, "There is power, power, wonder-working power in the blood of the Lamb." The demons hated that song. I could feel their absolute contempt rise up inside my mind.

"Shut up," the demons growled. "You'll be sorry, our master will send reinforcing devils to kill you," the evil devil threatened.

One devil spit foamy spittle out on the floor. The demons knew exactly who my deliverance ministers were spiritually and the power that they possessed. The demons believed and trembled that the ministers were connected to the superior power of Jesus Christ and that they had to obey their commands.

The ministers looked beyond my words and spoke directly to the spirits and said, "You have no power here. We bind you in the name of Jesus and command you to hold your peace and come out of him."

The authority of Jesus was more powerful. He cast out the legion in the Bible. The demons groveled, yelled, and struggled at the commands of my ministers. When the devils have been invited in, they have to be driven out, forcefully. They were wrenching me and ripping my guts out.

"We have a lot of churches here," the pastor said.

"Humph," said the evil demon, "churches don't bother us. Many of them are now powerless and many have joined the darkness. Only a few are still believing the Bible and hardly a person realizes this power."

A demon called Lazarus said, "Besides, we own the town."

Then I heard a strange cry pouring from my throat—a discordant mixture of two voices—one of holy anger, one of terror. Neither resembled my own.

"Be still and hold your mouth, you are a foul wicked devil," said the minister. His voice had raised two pitches.

"We are not interested in your stupid plans. We know what the Guru told us about you and your dumb plans. We are going too win."

"Yuk!" the demon said in disgust, "*&&^*&^." He was using the foulest language.

"Shut up and be gone in Jesus name!" one of the ministers said firmly. The evil spirit was fully manifested.

"No, no, no, I won't go." The demon was trembling in my body and my hands were pushed forward like cats' claws, ready for attack. The demon was looking out of my eyes and fixed now on the ministers. I could feel the thing definitely bulging with fear and loathing. It was a sight from hell.

The minister spoke directly to me. "Vagalas, ask Jesus to help you, call out his name and renounce the powers of darkness."

"No!" I screamed and shook my head.

Then the demon took over my voice again. "Leave me alone, you &*&^^%," the demon swore, "fool. He's mine." Someone put a handkerchief in my mouth to stop the demon's insulting words.

"Keep your mouth shut and hold your peace. You will not wrench him. We forbid you to continue your demonic manifestations. Our power is greater than this evil force!"

Removing the handkerchief from my mouth, a minister spoke directly to me. "Vagalas, you must renounce it," the minister pressed me.

"No, I can't . . . " The words trailed away incoherently. I gave a look of half-startled wariness and then a sharp scream escaped from my throat.

Oh, how those demons hated the touch of Jesus. The preachers' hands were like burning coals on my head. My body was rigid, now drenched in perspiration. My eyes were no longer focusing while the veins stood out on my neck pulsating rapidly. Foam dribbled from my mouth but I tried to keep it tightly shut to keep the evil spirits from escaping. The spirits were really stirred-up as she continued to press them to leave. This battle was intense.

The minister spoke, "I am not afraid, you demons can scream and shout. You don't scare me. I know who I am in Christ," the minister returned in a tone of voice one might use to reprimand a dog.

"It's so dark out there. So dark and so forever," the demon's voice was alien, intimidating. "Please don't make me leave." It was whiney.

No longer looking at him, my face turned to one side and looked at the wall. I feared for my mind and life. My will was the last bastion of bondage. For a while the demon was rather belligerent with him, but as the minister took authority over it, a tremor came into the demon's voice. Then, I became weak and limp. I was so weak that I could not lift the Bible that had been placed on my stomach.

Someone anointed my forehead with oil.

That minister was forceful and the demons reacted violently. "Shut up and obey the name of Jesus. You have no power here," the minister commanded the demon to weaken.

The oil felt as though a hot sizzling poker iron every time she touched me with it. Then he pried my mouth open and poured some of that oil down my throat.

"You stop that you fool..." Struggling to get free.

It was impossible. They had me totally bound. The ministers' eyes watched the reactions of the devil. According to Romans 8:37, "We are more than conquerors through Him that loved us."

Giant beads of sweat were pouring out of my pores. "Please, leave me alone. I don't want to go," it whimpered now. "This is my home. I've been here a long time. I was here when Vagalas was born. He was promised," the demon pleaded.

"Be quiet," the pastor said.

He was full of defeat and fear and I could feel it. There was a suffocating blackness hovering above me, feeling as if I had wrestled an invisible prince of darkness like a battle against nameless dread.

"Depart! Unclean spirit. In the name of Jesus, depart! Go!" officially pronounced the minister. He instantly experienced victory and the Lord's power.

"Can't you understand that he belongs to me?" the demon murmured in disgust. "This is my home. I've been here since before he was born." He trembled at the sound of the name of Jesus and the minister's commands.

Then foam began to seep out of the corner of my mouth and I became violent, kicking, jerking and extremely strong.

"In the name of Jesus . . . In the name of Jesus . . ." the people sang. The demons shouted. "Shut up, shut up,"

I covered my ears, trying to block out the words. Somebody was reading the Bible. This was absolutely driving the demons mad. They groaned, moaned, cringed and blinked. I heard my own voice speaking, coming from deep down in my belly.

"Help me, help me—Don't stop. This was my own spiritual voice speaking. "I'm bound. The demons have me bound in here." My body stiffened. Then my arms and legs stretched.

At first, the minister thought it was the voice of a demon. "Get out, I don't want to talk to you," the minister said firmly.

My emotions were really panicky. My voice was shaky but my voice came through "Please, don't stop. Help me," the words whipped like steel between them.

Freeing a person from the powers of darkness can sometimes, be fairly easy. However, it can also, at other times be exceedingly difficult. Degree of demonization is a factor as well as the person's will agreeing for the demon's departure. Remember I had been under demonic powers all my life.

"Jesus!" The cry ripped my throat.

My eyes flickered rapidly behind my tightly closed lids. Sweat had formed a glistening film on my forehead and temples. Then a pitch black hole consumed me. Whenever a person comes out of wizardry or witchcraft, the demon of death will try to kill them during deliverance sessions. Their eyes will sink into the back of their heads and you can only see the whites showing. They will have difficulty breathing. The demons will tighten its grip around their throats. The person seems to be suspended between two worlds. This can be a very frightening matter to the deliverance minister if he or she is inexperienced. When this demon manifests, the session is very close to the end. I've never personally witnessed a demon killing someone during a deliverance session. And so, I survived this death demon too.

Abruptly a minister placed his hands on my shoulders. He was tired of listening to that stupid demon brag about his power. He fully intended to show him who had more power. Jesus is still alive today, the same as He was yesterday and that He will be tomorrow. At that moment, a fresh fire, a supernatural anointing came upon him by the Holy Ghost and he gazed into my terrorized eyes.

"Come out of him, in Jesus' name," then forcefully, "you will loose him now!" His voice was echoing in my ears. I felt trapped in my head. Instantly, all the remaining evil demons came rushing out causing a yellow, stinking slime to vomit out of my throat. The minister fought becoming nauseated. This disgusting sight was enough to drive the hardest heart into the arms of Jesus.

In terror, "Sure, the devil has power," said the pastor victoriously, "but Jesus Christ has more." The demons were leaving. I coughed, belched and sniffed.

Everyone was saying, "Praise the Lord. Thank you, Jesus."

The battle is truly the Lord's. When the last demon came out with a loud piercing scream, I instantly knew that I was free. I felt drained, tried and empty. My body was wet with sweat yet I felt weak, light, and a little dizzy. This battle had lasted all night!

Finally the minister said, "I command all these devils to go where the Lord Jesus Christ sends you. I forbid that you can ever return to Vagalas as long as he lives. I place you under the authority of Jesus Christ Who is "far above all powers."

All of a sudden, there was a still silence. It was a beautiful, holy hush that exists when the Holy Spirit is present. I was weeping. Joy filled my soul. I was free! His Presence was so precious. I was clean and then the Holy Spirit gave me a heart of flesh. The coldness of my heart was washed away by the touch of God. However, I was very tired and drained. My body knew that it had been through a battle.

My pastor laid his hands on my head and prayed for the Holy Spirit to come and fill the empty places. All at once it was peaceful.

At the same time, I was engulfed in the Holy Spirit's fire. I felt so overflowing with excitement. When the Holy Spirit came rushing in, I felt wonderful, truly, totally free at last. I looked around. Everything looked so clean. I felt alive and vibrant. Whenever the Holy Spirit took possession of my body, He filled me with Himself and the joy of the Lord bubbled forth from my mouth. My hands shot up into the air praising God with all my might.

Today, I am a new creature in Christ and have a new garment, singing a new song and don't wear witches' robes anymore. I have a new robe of righteousness (Isaiah 61:10). Once the Spirit has touched you, you can never look back!

After the Holy Spirit came, He began revealing the Word of God to me. I had such a hunger for the Word that every waking minute was spent consuming the Bible. It became my strength. There was an explosion of spiritual fervor and a fire that blazed in my bones. I will never be the same again! When it was over, the ministers continued to pray warfare prayers.

They anointed the room, bound the evil spirits and commanded every demonic force to leave and never return! There was so much peace that I cannot describe it to you. I can tell you this. As a result, I am free by the power of Jesus Christ!

Chapter Five

Life After Deliverance

And after all that is come upon us for our evil deeds, and for our great trespass, seeing that thou our God hast punished us less than our iniquities deserves, and hast given us such deliverance as this. (Ezra 9:13)

PERSECUTION

At a point in time, I got disturbed because I was going through a lot of persecution. Many Christians simply could not believe that Jesus would save a wizard. Some were frightened while others said that I was crazy. I was being bruised, hurt, and rejected.

Voices were whispering in my ears, "Why don't you just return to Guru (Satan), Vagalas. He doesn't hate you like those rebellious people do."

The spiritual warfare was intense. I was tempted and becoming very confused. Then one night, the Man appeared to me again and said, "I have called you." His presence comforted me. He ministered and encouraged me. Thank God that my pastor stood with me. I never would have made it without him. It was not popular. Many simply left his church.

He told the people, "Look, what you are doing to this gentleman, you had better be very careful if it is of the Lord, and it will surely stand. So don't fight against the Spirit of God."

I began going into the streets of Ghana. I would preach to the people about Jesus because that is all that I knew. God used me to do many supernatural signs and wonders. People had all kinds of curses and diseases. However I worked with Jesus while many Christian people continued to reject me and gossiped. I nearly gave up.

If somebody had told me about Christ, I could have gone to that person and asked, "My friend, is this how Christians act toward new converts? I won't come again." However, nobody told me about Jesus. I could not go to anyone. I couldn't blame anyone. I couldn't say, "You told me to give my life to Jesus and look at what is happening to me." The Man was becoming my hope.

I did not understand what was happening to me. I felt spiritually crushed and wounded by so many fellow Christians. The demons of hell hounded me. They tried to bring fear and torment. Truthfully, whenever a high level witch or wizard converts into the Body of Christ, many well-meaning Christians will stir against those kinds of people. They believe that they are doing the work of God.

However, my pastor and Jesus were always standing with me and encouraging me to continue. It was only later that I was able to forgive the Christians that were rejecting me and persecuting me. This could only happen with biblical maturity. Luke 8: 34 describes the reaction of the people to the power of God. The Word says that they fled! They talked about it and all the people came out of curiosity to see if it were true. When they came they saw the man who was previously possessed by a legion of demons sitting in peace at the feet of Jesus, fully clothed and of a sound mind and they were afraid!

They feared the power of Jesus and had not even witnessed the demons expelled!

FULL GOSPEL BUSINESSMEN

This same spirit of rejection and fear followed me until a man called Demos Shakarian of the Full Gospel Businessmen International Fellowship came to Africa. He was looking for local people who had interesting conversion testimonies to be given in the hotels.

Someone said, "I know this tall African who was a former witch doctor. He has a testimony that is so grave that when people hear him, they are so frightened, they faint and many run out of the church."

One of the American men said, "Go get him."

They sent for me because they were curious about my testimony When I appeared before them, I asked if they were sure they wanted to listen to my testimony. I told them that when I told my story in church some people would run out and others would faint. I asked them, "If I tell you will you collapse?"

Demos Shakarian laughed and prayed with me.

I told him my testimony.

He said, "I like it. I think it is really good. Can you share this testimony as a speaker in our meetings?"

I replied, "Yes."

For the first time I spoke to a crowd. I was so excited. The Bible says "They overcome Satan by the blood the Lamb, and by the word of their testimony" (Revelation 12:11).

In the beginning when I shared my testimony half of the people left, but I ignored them and continued to speak. Gradually my story began to spread and pastors called me to minister in their churches. Then Christians began to accept my ministry. They believed that I was telling them the truth because when I prayed for the sick and demon possessed wonderful things happened. Jesus healed every type of illness and the people were being set free. Even witch doctors began to come in search of freedom. They reasoned that if I could get delivered maybe they could be free too. When I prayed for them in the name of Jesus they would vomit up spirits shaped in the form of snakes and other things. Many people were healed and delivered.

The pastors began to say, "This is of God because for about three or four years, Vagalas is still living for Jesus Christ, so let us protect him. They prayed and decided to ordain me. They could see the call upon my life. We can teach him and correct him."

It was after the support of Christian leadership that I started enjoying Christian life. I loved being in the ministry. Speaking requests began to pour in and I found myself speaking all over the country. My life started getting better. I discovered that many Christians were interested in the power of Jesus that had delivered this tall man from deep witchcraft from the powers of the devil.

POWERS OF THE WORLD

Besides worldwide powers, Satan has assigned specific ruling spirits over geographical areas such as nations, states, communities, groups, churches, families, and over every individual. Satan can choose from a wide array of spirits. In a single city alone, one neighborhood could be under the spirit of gambling, sexual perversions and still another under alcohol. For instance, Nevada could be under a spirit of gambling, and the spirit of poverty could be ruling in places in Africa.

Another tactic Satan uses to defeat a Christian is the lack of knowledge. This is one of the strongest weapons that he is using now. The Bible says, "My people are destroyed for a lack of knowledge" (Hosea4:6).

If you go to the Book of Ephesians, Chapter 6 verse 12, says, "We wrestle not against flesh and blood but against principalities, against powers, against the rulers of the darkness of this world and against spiritual wickedness in higher places."

Satan has divided the world into geographical areas over which he has placed ruling spirits or strongmen. These ruler spirits control the spiritual activities with their assigned boundaries.

Look at Deuteronomy 7:1: "When the LORD thy God shall bring thee into the land whither thou goest to possess it, and hath cast out many nations before thee, the Hittites, and the Girgashites, and the Amorites, and the Canaanites, and the Perizzites, and the Hivites, and the Jebusites, seven nations greater and mightier than thou."

Satan has a clever plan or scheme for every person in the world. He is the head of all evil opposing forces. He controls all negative powers. He is the head of the satanic forces described in Ephesians 6:12. There are four all-important divisions of his kingdom that are well organized. When we leave his office and come down to the next level, we will see Principalities. Then we will see Powers. Then we will see Rulers of Darkness and finally spiritual Wickedness in high places. Satan's kingdom is very well organized. The work of Principalities manages the forces and dominions dealing with nations and governments. The second level is Powers. They have authority and power of action in all the spheres open to them.

The third level, World Rulers are governing the darkness and blindness of the world at large. And finally, there are wicked spirits in heavenly places which are the forces being directed in and upon the Church of Jesus Christ. These wicked spirits put into action wiles, fiery darts, attacks, and every imaginable deception about doctrine that they are capable of planning.

When I got saved, the Lord told me that Satan binds many people in Africa. The Lord said, "Soon the entire world will be bound by him." Remembering the things that I witnessed as a wizard, I knew it was true.

NEW AGE OF AQUARIUS

I remember we went to another world conference. Satan (Guru) told us that he was aiming his control over the governments. He said that when he wins the governments, he would get control of the people. He revealed a plan to put his own people at the top of governments. He told us that his people would change the laws to suit his plans. He told us, "The Age of the Fish is over. We are moving into the New Age of Aquarius. Our goal in the new world will be to root out all that worship of God."

Guru saw himself as god. He saw himself as the mighty, ruling the New World Order. He prophesied that a new dawn would soon appear and he would create a new Eden where there would be peace and safety. He saw the planet turning green the waterways clean, the trees waving their healthy branches at him, the air marvelous to breathe again. He envisioned every soul on the face of the earth bowing, worshiping him for his unbelievable management of the planet. He saw masses of people dying. Those were the faceless ones. These people are those who were ones to be sent into another dimension by the demons to cleanse the world from their cancerous minds for not receiving his ruling power. Even the nature gods were bowing to him. He spoke to us of a picture of his perfect world as it would be in just the days ahead.

"I am a god. I am a god!" he shouted enthusiastically, his hands stretched forward. His face was flushed. He was preaching his new religion. "I am the god!" he shouted wildly. His eyes were flashing, his hands pumping. Everyone bowed and worshiped him. We followed his every whim in zombie-style fashion.

One of the leaders of the world stood and said, "People keep saying, we need a leader. Yes, we are looking for a messiah. We are looking for someone that we can follow wholeheartedly. Give us a new avatar (spiritual man)—if he is a man or beast—we will follow him." Everyone stood to their feet and cheered and applauded.

Who would believe me if I got on a national television program and said these things? I'd be marked as a crazy man. Who could receive the message that New Age theology can be summed up in the two lies of Satan in the Garden of Eden (Genesis 3)? The first lie is "You shall not surely die" (reincarnation).

The second is as Satan promised: "You shall be as gods" (self-realization; all you need, you'll find within). These two demonic lies are part of nearly every cult and pagan religion in the world. It is the battleground for the minds of men. When Satan has captured the mind, he can get the spirit. The battle lines are drawn on every front. It is happening in country after country.

Lastly, who could believe the New Age includes the full-fledged worship of Lucifer? Certainly not one Christian that I know would believe that there is a group of international conspirators who are not only moving to create a New World Order but also fashioning a New Universal Religion.

MANIPULATION OF HUMANS

My life was saturated spiritually but from the occult point of view. To me, it was puzzling that the majority of humankind does not believe there are spiritual beings. It was also baffling that most Christians were blinded to these demons that were presently affecting their daily lives. The truth is, here are spiritual beings (Satan and the fallen angels now demons) that not only affect humankind, but they also have the ability to deceive and manipulate humankind from the spiritual realm. In other words, it is difficult for the average human being to believe that demons exist. However the fact that they did not believe nor perceive that these spiritual beings exist, enabled the wizards and witches, together with the invisible beings, to manipulate masses more easily because they were helpless to defend themselves.

I knew that throughout the world a paranormal phenomenon was profoundly manifesting. All facets of the human society had confronted these unexplained paranormal phenomena. Satan taught us that whenever human beings experience paranormal phenomena, the majority of these people become compelled to believe these are coming from a benevolent god. Therein lies the great deception because the Ascended Masters (powerful high level demons) were beginning to make their presences known to the masses.

A HEART OF FLESH

After my conversion, I cried and wept for my people, because I knew the terrible plans that would soon come to pass. "Lord, I want to do something to help my motherland." I had to start in Africa—my homeland, it had to be a strong start or it wouldn't work. I began my ministry gradually by the grace of God, I am here today, telling you my story. This is what the Lord has done for me.

Chapter Six

My New Life

But the anointing which ye have received of him abideth in you, and ye need not that any man teach you: but as the same anointing teacheth you of all things, and is truth, and is no lie, and even as it hath taught you, ye shall abide in him. (1 John 2:27)

NEW LIFE

After my baptism, the Lord changed my name to Samuel. God was doing many tremendous things in my ministry. People were getting saved, baptized in the Holy Spirit, and receiving the greatest experiences with Jesus. They were getting set free from evil spirits. My name was beginning to spread throughout the city. Many people started seeking me out to minister to them. It was wonderful to see the Lord using me in such a powerful way. I was so grateful that He trusted me and used me to change people's lives from the darkness into His marvelous light. My wife, Evelyn, is a beautiful woman. I thank Jesus for giving me such a wonderful spiritual mate. She was always willing to stand with me and has become a powerful prayer warrior for my ministry. She is also an evangelist and has planted many churches in Africa. In addition, she became a devoted wife and mother to our three beautiful children, Esther, Samuel and Philip.

EVELYN'S STORY

My wife's mother left her father when she was very young. One night her mother just slipped away in the night and disappeared.

Someone told her where she could find her mother. She also slipped away into the night and went to her mother. Her mother had married another man who was a Muslim. He was a chief in the village. He loved Evelyn as his own daughter, adopted and educated her. However, she was required to become a Muslim. She was attending the university when suddenly she went physically blind. Some of the students told her there is a man who is speaking at the Full Gospel Businessmen's meeting who was doing miracles and "maybe he could restore your eyesight. She attended the meeting where she met a man called Samuel Vagalas Kanco. I prayed for her and cast the devils out that were blinding her. "Praise the Lord God Almighty," she whispered. Her eyes crossed involuntarily for a moment, and then began to focus. "I can see," she shouted. Her eyes caught mine and I could see the light of Jesus Christ in them. Her tears gushed forth as I took a cloth and wiped her eyes.

"You will never be the same again," I said.

"My sweet Lord..." she said sniffling, "He..." her words began to slur. Then unintelligent words burst forward. The Holy Spirit had immersed her in His Baptism and she was worshiping the King of Glory for the victory. His presence was precious. Then the mood changed and the crowed began to shout with cheers for Jesus.

She was a wonderful, lovely lady. She squeezed my hand so tightly that my fingers lost their circulation. "Oh," she said breathlessly, "if only you could feel what I feel. Do you see that light that is watching me?" Tears were freely flowing down her cheeks. She felt the presence of Jesus in the room, no doubt about it. Looking up, she could sense a crowd of witnesses in the room. She could hear the angels singing with her spirit. The music was more splendorous than any other note that she'd ever heard on this earth. What she was feeling was the Lord touching her spirit and changing her heart. Jesus was giving her a heart of flesh. Something had touched my heart that day too. Although I had ministered to hundreds of women, this woman had some kind of meaningful attraction to me. Of course, at that moment, I did not know that I was touching my future wife with the power of faith. In spite of her powerful emotions, the Spirit of God dominated the room with peace, far beyond the ability of my words to describe. Something was happening and until this moment, I had never thought about doing anything with my life except serving Jesus.

We became close spiritual friends. Evelyn's spiritual growth began to abound with commitment and spiritual wisdom. We began to spend our spare time together. Her family was totally against her seeing me. To them, I was just a poor preacher without any hope of a future. I struggled with my feelings for her but I knew that she was a precious gift from God. I felt His blessing upon my intentions of asking her to become my bride. I loved her. Several years later, we were married. Evelyn's heart was set on me and she trusted God that He would rescue me and make me a success. She worked hard in the beginning of our marriage while I studied and witnessed in the streets of Ghana. She is the light of my life and I've always felt that she's the greatest blessing of my life. God has blessed us. My brothers have converted to the Lord and are working in the ministry. Evelyn's mother and grandmother have converted from the Muslim faith. Evelyn tells about her mother's conversion from the Muslim religion. Her mother came for a visit. Evelyn was witnessing to a couple of witches about the reality of Jesus.

She suddenly turned to her mother and said, "This woman is a great woman of God." One of the witches replied, "not so, we could kill her in a second, but someone is praying for her."

Evelyn turned to her mother and said, "Did you hear that? They can kill you in a second but my prayers are protecting you? Well, you'd better turn your life over to Jesus Christ because I'm not praying for you any more."

She laughs when she tells the rest of the story. She stopped praying for her mother. Several days later, her mother came to her and begged her to pray for Jesus to forgive her. She became a Christian because of the torment that was happening to her mother.

Her grandmother became saved seven years later. She had been saved about seven days when Dr. Pat Holliday came to Ghana. Dr. Holliday asked her if she wanted to receive Jesus Christ as her personal Savior. She said that she had already asked Him to save her. Then Dr. Holliday placed her hands on both mother and grandmother's head and rebuked the Muslim spirits. Instantly they were both freed and received the Baptism of the Holy Spirit with the evidence of speaking with other tongues.

Something else happened too. My Grandmother was bent over to the waist. At this time she was eighty years old. Instantly, her back was straightened by the power of God! We give God the glory that he is also working in our families.

EVANGELISM

We started as an evangelistic ministry in the Assemblies of God. At the same time, Evelyn was working and we were hardly holding our lives together. Believe me, we ate a lot of rice during those years while I attended Bible College and going into the streets to witness. I was getting a lot of people saved; delivered and healed. I was trained by the pastors of the Assembly of God and will always be grateful for their wonderful Christian friendship. I still have a very warm relationship with my old pastor. He has always encouraged me. God bless him and my many other Christian brothers who have blessed my ministry over the years. After about ten years the Lord led me out of the Assembly of God to establish a church called the Lord's Vineyard Chapel International. Our churches have no affiliation with any of the Vineyard churches in America.

The Lord's Vineyard is a church that was called into existence by the Spirit of God. We have a membership of more than thirty thousand people. He saw the need to develop this work for the purpose of teaching about the power of God and exposing the powers of Satan. I believe that God wants to spread the message of freedom to his believers as well as the announcement to unbelievers that deliverance is available to them I have been blessed by God to train many men and women in the ministry of deliverance. Whenever I travel to evangelize the work goes on just as if I were there. There are more than forty trained ministers who work in our Bible school and the Lord's Vineyard's International Chapel.

My beautiful wife, Evelyn, also works in the ministry. Thank God for a wonderful, holy woman. God has trained her to preach and stand with me in the ministry. She is a phenomenal mother to our three children. In fact, she is a brilliant minister who is totally devoted to the Lord's cause. For instance she has successfully trained hundreds of women to pray and fast.

Believe me, when this army moves into action, the devils tremble. Her prayers, I believe, have marked our ministry for great success. We have planted more than twenty-five churches in Africa, two in London and two in Canada. I was ordained Bishop over these churches in 1999. God is blessing our work and we are truly an international ministry.

My vision is that God will use us to help bring our nation from idolatry to the reality that Jesus Christ is Lord. There are so many other visions that I have. One is the establishment of a Christian hospital in my city, Accra. You see the Muslims own and operate all hospitals. Regrettably, whenever someone gets sick they are forced to convert to that faith in order to get in the hospital! We are operating two medical clinics to try to overcome this problem. Another vision is that someone gave me a double-topped mountain. I want to build a minister's retreat. It will have constant intercessory prayer, twenty-four hours a day. I see a place where ministers from over the world can come and rest. They can receive new anointing while prayer arises from the sides of the mountain.

I also envision our churches being planted across Africa. I believe this will happen with the blessings and grace of God. The Lord is also blessing the churches in Canada, and the churches in London.

MY DREAM

Africa must be free from the physical bondage of dependency upon others for its prosperity. Her people can rise up and take their places in the creation of a new and flourishing nation when they learn about Jesus Christ and His Word. As a result, He will back up His Word. In particular, He will bless them by delivering them from the generational curses. These curses always arrive when the practice of idolatry exists. Also, because of this, God is raising many ministers who are mighty warriors against the powers of darkness. These messengers are going to set spiritual captives free and deliver cities. This is my vision, that the people in Africa are released from obligations, from the entrapments of spiritual bondage, and blindness of idolatry. Jesus will make their lives better just as surely as He made my life better.

Chapter Seven

Living for Jesus

Afterward Jesus findeth him in the temple, and said unto him, Behold, thou art made whole: sin no more, lest a worse thing come unto thee. (John 5:14)

SIN, A THING OF THE PAST

In my country, once a person becomes born again, they hardly ever return to their sin life. The reason is that the leadership of the church really goes after them if they backslide. Another matter, if a Christian backslides in Africa, they are open to strong-serious demonic attack by the witches and wizards. These evil agents quickly rush in and try to kill them before they can repent. First they will tempt him or her to do wrong. As the cold Christian obeys, he or she becomes open for a spirit to enter and take control. Secondly, if the sin is continually indulged in after professed conversion, not repented, such a person is wide open to demonic oppression in its many forms. In this way, Satan's agents (witches and wizards) can see their spiritual condition and quickly move to take control. In other words, spiritual discerning of spirits is needed to help protect these weak people. Moreover, we try to bring them to repentance. It is very dangerous and delusional to think Satan's demons adopt a hands off policy to believers. In fact, they can affect and afflict believers. They buffet them, oppose and seek to tempt or deceive and lead them astray. To sum up, they look for and quickly seize any advantage to hinder believers.

The good news is that Jesus came to destroy the works of the devil (1 John 3:8). Indeed, He did just that when He said, "The thief cometh not, but for to steal, and to kill, and to destroy: I am come that they might have life, and that they might have it more abundantly" (John 10:10).

HISTORY

I believe that many of the problems that we face in Africa are due to the curses that come down generational lines due to the worship of other gods. These curses are found in the Bible. We didn't know anything about God. We did not have any connection with Jehovah. Man is created in such a way that he has to have God. There is a place inside him that only the Spirit of God can fill. In the absence of the true God, the Devil came to fill our hearts. My people fell in love with the Devil and so we put our trust in Him by giving him our souls, spirits and bodies. We went very deep and were led to worship trees, rocks and rivers, etc. Because of this, we began to think like trees and rocks. The Devil took advantage of our spiritual ignorance and had his evil grip and planted his seed in every African family. Just as Christians who believed in the Bible designed America's Constitution, our culture was ruled by idolatrous people and designed by the Devil. Since our culture was charted by the Devil, many of our people grew to be like the Devil. The Devil has no friend. Whether you serve him or not, he will try to destroy you. He gave Africa a lot of misery such as sickness, death, and poverty. These are the evil gifts you will find in the heart of Africa. The Devil has no peace or joy, so he cannot give these gifts to his people. He gave us what he has, utter poverty and destruction. Remember this. Development comes from Jesus, and where Jesus is, civilization always changes to a more advanced stage. Because of America's connection with Jesus, her people were also blessed to think like Jesus. So your people had the power to think, prosper, and were able to give the world great inventions. America is also called the breadbasket of the world. God blessed American. Christian churches sent missionaries all over the world. I would still be in idolatry if the Christians had not responded to the call of God.

We are praying for America because it has been the lighthouse of the world concerning the truth of Jesus Christ as the Savior of the world. If that beacon fire goes out, the entire world will go into darkness. America has enjoyed life, peace and joy but Jesus was not in Africa, there was little advancement and it was called the Dark

Continent. I am a man with a vision for my country and it's a vision of spiritual freedom and prosperity for Africa. Many of my people are still steeped deeply in witchcraft powers.

Every nation in which these forms of witchcraft are practiced is cursed with poverty and oppression spiritually, physically, and politically. The people are demonized and controlled by the powers of darkness. Considering that my people were serving these shrines and strange gods, the Biblical principle that a foreign land will enslave the people came into force. These curses must come to pass because the Bible says that God is no respecter of persons. Therefore, because we were serving strange gods, the Scripture was fulfilled in Africa. It was not easy at that time for the white men to leave their countries in small boats to come to Africa. They forged ahead through winds and storms sailing the oceans at great peril to themselves to bring the Gospel to my country. You can see that it was a supernatural force pushing these foreign people to Africa.

It is interesting that at the same time that Abraham Lincoln liberated the blacks in America, missionaries from your nation began to bring the gospel to our people. During this period of time, my people were gradually turning to God. He said, "It is time to stop slavery." It happened because of supernatural power from God. These curses have followed the black race for centuries are there because the Devil was able to spiritually blind them through idol worship. The Bible is true. Even though they did not know

Jehovah, the Biblical curse concerning the worship of strange gods brought a curse of slavery.

Since the Scriptures must be fulfilled, the Americans and Europeans, with the help of African chiefs and Arab traders, captured millions of Africans. They were marked for slavery. My people became slaves in foreign lands. Through slavery however, many millions of African Americans and their descendants have been born again and will spend eternity in heaven and not hell. In the 1700s and 1800s the triangle trade was between Africa (slaves) and New England (molasses) and West Indies (sugar). So not only did the Southern sates benefit from slavery but also the Northern states and Europe. At one time, Mexico had the most African slaves of all the New World.

After centuries of struggle, the slave trade ended, but Europeans still wanted Africa's riches. They brought their guns and captured different parts of Africa, renamed them and sent their own people to rule over my people. After many years of war, Africans won their independence. Then two famous kingdoms were reclaimed. In 1957, Gold Coast became Ghana. In 1960 the French Sudan became Mali. Another period of Africa's heritage had begun. It opened our people's minds to believe for a greater future for Africa's culture. We could dream of a great civilization rising up from the ashes of our people's bondage, a country stepping into a new era.

Church Repentance

We are blessed in Ghana today. Our churches came together in repentance and through breaking covenants with the devil and denying our bellies, crying out to the Lord. We repented for all the evil atrocities that had been committed by our people by allowing demons and evil spirits to take possession of our city. We knew from the Bible that when people cry out to the Lord, He responds to them. Our government is a democracy. Our cities are filling with Christian Churches, mighty revivals are moving throughout our land. The Bible is true. It says that if a people worship strange gods of idolatry, they will become slaves in a foreign land. Our people did not know Jehovah. Still, the force of the law fell upon the heads of my ancestors. However, Jesus Christ is faithful. We African Christians are living testimonies of hope, just as He will help us to prosper. To God is the glory.

DOUBT AND SPIRITUAL BONDAGE

I realize that many pastors will read this book and just excuse this true testimony as false. In like manner, they will reason, "a Christian can't have a demon." Nevertheless, if you will read your Bible, you'll see that Jesus drove the evil spirits out before the person could follow Him. Indeed, He gave His followers the power to do the same miracles that He did (Matthew10: 8; Luke 9:1). Accordingly, the disciples did the same thing! They healed the sick and cast out devils.

Demons are real, spirits, individual beings. They are the instruments through which Satan attempts to consume and devour Christians on a daily basis. God has placed a supernatural invisible barrier in the lives of Christians, beyond which these demons cannot go. They must depend on the Christian to lower that barrier for them. The barrier is the "sovereign will" of the individual. This then makes it necessary for the demons to use lies, tricks, deceptions or any other underhanded means to defeat the Christian. Yes, demons are real! Satan is real! However, spiritual warfare is real only if the Bible is taken literally. Otherwise, different names are assigned to demonic problems. If the person should base his beliefs on supposition, he can believe whatever he wishes.

Satan is a master deceiver. He did not win! He became a defeated foe at Calvary. It is worth noting that Satan became a defeated foe only in the lives of those people who are willing to accept victory from Christ. Since Satan is a god (2 Corinthians 4:4), we must resist him each day with victory, which is the Word of God! Satan's attempt to consume Christians continues every day in the life of each Christian. This fact makes spiritual warfare a daily reality. We are not free from the fight! In the life of a Christian there is no such thing as neutral. If we do not win then we lose.

The Scriptures predict that there will be a great increase in demonic power in the last days. An increasing flood of evil, influencing society, the church and the world, characterizes our age. So the works and doctrines of evil seducing spirits have enslaved multitudes of people. As a result, these people are suffering mental, psychic, and spiritual demonic bondage. There are millions who have now been infected by these spiritual AIDS. In fact, they can be free if the Church will obey the Lord and cast them out! Only Christians have the authority and power to deliver them. In conclusion, the idea that evil spirits only operate in uncivilized parts of the world is false! God doesn't do everything. We are His co-workers. There is a part that we must do.

The Bible says, "The night is far spent, the day is at hand: Let us therefore cast off the works of darkness, and let us put on the armor of light. Let us walk honestly, as in the day; not in rioting and drunkenness, not in immorality and wantonness (debauchery), not in strife and envying, but put ye on the Lord Jesus Christ, and make not provision for the flesh, to fulfill the lusts thereof." (Romans 13:12–14).

Positive action is required. The Apostle Paul is writing here to a Christian body of believers just like you and me. He's not writing to pagans. These believers were into the works of darkness. Some of them were still hanging onto past or pet sins. If that is the case in our lives, we must cast off those things that pull us down spiritually.

"The Spirit of the Lord Jehovah is upon me; because Jehovah hath anointed me to preach good tidings unto the meek; he hath sent me to bind up the brokenhearted, to proclaim liberty to the captives, and the opening of the prison to them that are bound; to proclaim the acceptable year of Jehovah and the day of vengeance of our God; to comfort all that mourn; to appoint unto them that mourn in Zion, to give unto them beauty for ashes, the oil of joy for mourning, the garment of praise for the spirit of heaviness; that they may be called trees of righteousness, the planting of Jehovah, that he may be glorified!" (Isaiah 61:1–3).

The truth is, neither the Christian nor the unbeliever can safely cross over the forbidden lines of Satan's knowledge and remain free. Most important, the Church of Jesus Christ is alive! Most important, His church can deliver the captives and set them free by His name and authority.

Isaiah said, "I heard the voice of the Lord saying: 'Whom shall I send, and who will go for Us?' Then I said, here am I! Send me" (Isaiah 6:8).

Chapter Eight

Awakening the Great Giant

For rebellion is as the sin of witchcraft, and stubbornness is as iniquity and idolatry. Because thou hast rejected the word of the LORD, he hath also rejected thee from being king. (1 Samuel 15:23).

WITCHES AND WIZARDS' WORK

To take Satan's territory, you must have a broken heart for the people. My heart is broken because I have experienced the wicked entrapments of Satan. Especially since I experienced the bondage of witchcraft and idolatry, I know its slavery and wickedness. In fact, I believe that our faith is a living faith. Likewise, His churches can change people, cities and nations. Indeed, My prayer is that Christ's power will be fully known throughout the African continent.

Africa is a continent of many gods such as the trees, rocks, rivers, paganism, Mohammed; and of many spirits, the demons of magic, witchcraft and soothsaying; and the true God of Christianity. It contains some 6,000 tribes. In fact, so complex are African races, cultures, languages and religions that anthropologists cannot agree about many facts that are available to them. Even so, there are certain basic concepts, which underlie all African religions. These concepts far from being the mumbo jumbo popularly associated with witch doctors, black magic, fetishes, jujus and the rest of it, are still powerful social forces. The Church of Jesus Christ must awaken to the reality of evil spiritual agents. Their job is to rob, kill and destroy. The truth is we see people manifesting demons in our church services. Believe me, if they are in our services, they are in your services too!

DECEPTION

As a former high-level wizard, my job was to bewitch and deceive people. As a result, this was carried out by the power of magical potions that were conjured up in my wizard's pot. For instance, I was able to cast various kinds of spells, hexes and did blood sacrifices to carry through my goals. During this time, I had about ten eyes located around my head. In other words, I could see virtually everywhere at once. Whenever I looked at a person, I could see them no matter if they were in front, side or back me. I could see through them just as if they were being X-rayed. At this time, the spirits also, gave me the ability to change into five animals. Because of this my work was made more treacherous and dangerous. Using these various forms enabled me to accomplish evil assignments without being noticed by human eyes. Actually I was able to watch them and report their plans back to Satan's Kingdom beneath the water. However, if a witch turns into an animal and is killed while in this form, their natural body will die!

Satan also uses his demons to turn into appearances of sea creatures such as octopuses, squids, crabs, sea serpents, mermaids, sea monsters, fish, etc. Over the years, in my deliverance ministry, I have personally witnessed many people under the powers of these spirits. Many times I have seen them manifesting in the manner of these sea creatures. You can, as a matter of fact, see them on the floor, swimming like a fish or hopping like a frog and then rolling around like a whale.

When Dr. Pat Holliday and her team came to Africa, she told me "they were amazed during deliverance sessions at the manifestations of the sea demons." She said that she had seen demons that were shaped like crabs, sea serpents, octopuses, squids, etc., over the course of her ministry. However, she did not understand the significance of them. She had never heard about marine spirits. That is, she had never heard of the witchcraft activity under the sea. Now I wonder about the popularity of the children's movies *The Little Mermaid* with its calypso music and *Nemo* with its charming little fish and creatures under the sea.

WITCHES & WIZARDS TEMPT CHRISTIANS?

Witches and wizards work through mind suggestions. They use humanly possessed people to sexually tempt the person to sin. They also use dreams. You must guard your dream life. They will use sexually explicit dreams. They will bring forms of dead people into your dreams, a husband or a wife, etc. They can bring a mate to you asking you to eat food. Christians must be careful with their nightlife because of the succubus (a male unclean spirit) or an incubus (a female unclean spirit) that comes at night to lie on the top of a sleeping person to have sexual intercourse with her or him.

As a protection to this demonic perversion, Christians should pray and place themselves under the Blood of Jesus around their houses and family every night. Ask for a hedge of protection and ask for guardian angels to protect them. Any sin breaks a hole in the hedge of protection and snakes (demons) can slither into the Christian's life. Every Christian must examine himself and if there is any unconfessed sin, he must confess quickly and place it under the blood of Jesus. Satan and his agents cannot defeat a Christian without that person giving them an open door (sin).

SEA AGENTS

There are psychic computers that track everyone on the earth. Their names and records are kept in the psychic computers. Assignments are given to Satan's agents to enforce the words of nations, cities and individuals that will fulfill the plans of Satan. The agents in the City under the Sea are constantly sent to control the plans of the government from the top to the bottom. We were sent to work for those candidates who walk in agreement with Satan's plans. I remember the various assignments that were carried out when I was a wizard. Therefore, after I became a Christian, I began to speak to my brothers and sisters about the powers of darkness. We began to come together in prayer and fasting. We denied ourselves and lay on our bellies day and night seeking freedom for our city and country. Demons do vary in wickedness. According to the Word, "Then goeth he, and taketh with himself seven other spirits more wicked than himself, and they enter in and dwell there: and the last state of that man is worse than the first. Even so shall it be also unto this wicked generation" (Matthew 12:45). We really do have the keys to the door of liberty to release Satan's captives. It pleases me to tell you that we have Christians at the top of our government. We enjoy much peace in our city because of this spiritual change in the spiritual realm. To God be the glory.

SPIRITUAL EYES MUST OPEN

The Bible says, "But strong meat belongeth to them that are of full age, even those who by reason of use have their senses exercised to discern both good and evil" (Hebrews 5:14). Yes, the gift of discerning of spirits, both good and bad, is vital to the church today, for many have "crept in unawares" (Jude 4). In Acts 16:16–18 we are shown a young girl possessed with a spirit of divination. She used it as a professional fortuneteller. She followed Paul and his workers for several days. In fact, she was giving out the following prophecy; "These men are the servants of the Most High God, which show us the way of salvation" (Acts 16:17). Her message was true they were Godly men who were taking the gospel to the lost. Nevertheless, her message was coming from the wrong source of supernatural power. She was empowered by a spirit of divination or a demon.

People who are being used by divination spirits should not be allowed to address a Christian congregation. The appointed leader must be able to see spiritually exactly what spirit is operating behind the human personality. The minister should be able to discern the deception of the supernatural force. Since the apostle Paul was able to see spiritually through the gift of discerning of spirits, he was able to see the evil spirit at work behind the woman's human personality.

After following Paul for several days, he was grieved and turned and said to the spirit, "I command thee in the name of Jesus to come out of her!" The Word of God continues, "And HE came out the same hour!" (Acts 16:18). "And he" shows that Paul was not speaking to the girl but the supernatural demon in her. HE was a spiritual being controlling her. Although invisible, HE was speaking through the girl's lips giving out a message to the people. Paul simply looked beyond the girl speaking flattering words and rebuked the demon. He knew that he had the responsibility to present the truth and protect the people. He dealt with this spirit by using his delegated superior power, the Name of Jesus, and it left. Jesus' power is always greater. The Bible shows Him victorious over Satan. "And having spoiled principalities and powers, he made a shew of them openly, triumphing over them in it" (Colossians 2:15). The war is already won in Christ who is not only our Lord but also Lord of all.

Like Paul, if we do our part, God will do His and He will give us power to chase demons. In our time many witches and wizards are being used by Satan to infiltrate Christian churches. They are only successful if the leadership is spiritually blinded or if there is sin in the camp. They are sent to destroy the church. Young, beautiful girls and boys are used to tempt in the realm of sexual sin. Many are used to spread slander and gossip to divide church members from the leadership. Others are used to bring bewitching doctrines and lying spirits to confuse the members. They are used as watchers to report back to the spirit leadership below the waters. Satan's agents can see and discern the spiritual state of Christians.

Honestly, they can tell if a Christian is really living for Jesus. To go into detail, there is a circle of light around the head, and a bright light that shines from their hearts. In addition, there is a great barricade of fire around the Christian. This wall of fire makes it impossible for an agent to get close to a Christian. Likewise, the genuine Christian has angels protecting them. There is one to the left and one to right and one behind. These angels guard them day and night. A witch can see the two angels that stand to their side, having two twisting swords in both hands. Accordingly, these swords are constantly being hurled around and around. That is, as long as the Christian is living a holy life. These swords began to slow down when the Christian sins and this is the time when a demon will try to rush to get in.

HOW AGENTS WORK IN CHURCHES

Satan's agents attend churches all the time. Consequently, they use powers to make people sleep and slumber during the teaching of the Word. Also, they make babies cry, make the equipment break and place disturbing thoughts in the minds of the people. They do anything that will distract the people from hearing the Word. Satan uses his agents, beautiful girls or handsome young boys, to seduce the preachers and church members. They use their bewitchments upon his or her family members or people in the congregation. For instance, these agents are also used to discourage other Christians. Likewise, they attack the preacher's character, and his family through slander and gossip. Furthermore, they will question the Word to bring doubt and unbelief. They will cause strife and disagreements. They will use powers of enchantments to twist the Word. Finally, they will deceive, blind and dull the hearing of believers. You see that attainment of spiritual knowledge is doing spiritual warfare. These agents' jobs are to keep you in darkness. You must fight the battle of the Word to get the knowledge that you need to survive.

Shortly after I got saved, I realized that most Christians were very unaware of Satan's strategies. Many Christians taught messages concerning the Principalities, Powers, Ruler and Wicked Spirits in high places as shown in Ephesians 6:12. Conversely, they seemed to be just words. They were not real to many Christians. Moreover, they were also not enlightened concerning the evil spirits in the bush, the sky and in the City Under the Sea. Thank God that many are waking up to the great spiritual warfare and are joining us in prayer and fasting to conquer these evil powers so that they can set the captives free.

I recognized that Christians must be taught about supernatural powers before they enter into spiritual warfare. For instance author Peter Wagner cites the importance of knowing spiritual warfare. He tells of two Presbyterian ministers in Ghana who underestimated the enemy. Wagner writes in his book, *Territorial Spirits Wrestling with Dark Angels,* "One of the Presbyterian ministers, contrary to the warnings of the people in the area, ordered a tree which had been enshrined by Satanic priests to be cut down. On the day that the last branch of the tree was lopped off, the minister collapsed and died. The second minister commanded that a fetish shrine be demolished. When it was destroyed, he suffered a stroke."

So what happened here? Why did the ministers die? I can only tell you this. These ministers were probably totally unaware of the reality of witchcraft powers. Regrettably, they probably charged boldly into battle without being properly trained in spiritual warfare. The Bible says, "My people are destroyed for lack of knowledge: because thou hast rejected knowledge, I will also reject thee, that thou shall be no priest to me: seeing thou hast forgotten the law of thy God, I will also forget thy children" (Hosea 4:6).

Most important, they were probably charging into battle without their spiritual armor and without claiming the protection of the blood of Jesus. Like millions of Christians, they simply didn't discern that Satan really does have power. They probably cut that enshrined tree down believing it was just a local superstition and that therefore it had no supernatural power. You see that they were wrong. Only a superior power can overcome Satan's power. However, one has to know the power of Christ and His Word to overcome the power of Satan.

It is true that Christians have more power than Satan and his agents. Even so, the Christian must spiritually know it beyond a shadow of doubt. Many Christians are not supernaturally inclined because they serve Jesus traditionally. They do not see matters from a supernatural view. In contrast, witch doctors can see in the spiritual realms and are totally committed to Satan's cause. They walk deeply with their devils and obey them. For instance, they can see if a Christian possesses what he or she professes.

The knowledgeable witch doctor would never challenge an anointed Christian. That is because he would know the dangers of the satanic power boomeranging back upon him. If a wizard sends a curse or a spirit to a person that truly has Jesus in his/her heart, the curse will return to the sender. Satan does have convincing supernatural power to unbelievers. He has spiritual power over unbelievers through their commitment to them and his causes. The Bible reveals that Jesus Christ's power is superior to all the power of Satan. Amazingly, God's Word also discloses that Christians are able to overcome all the powers of Satan and his minions.

CAN WIZARDS CAST OUT EVIL SPIRITS?

No! Wizards and witches all pretend to cast out evil spirits and heal the sick by potions and magic. Notwithstanding, every person that goes into this power will end up demon possessed. Satan simply is able to steal their souls by giving them a promise. Remember, only real Christians are able to cast out evil spirits and heal the sick. Jesus Christ gives them this authority.

The Bible tells us: "And Jesus knew their thoughts, and said unto them, Every kingdom divided against itself is brought to desolation; and every city or house divided against itself shall not stand: And if Satan cast out Satan, he is divided against himself; how shall then his kingdom stand?" (Matthew 12:25-26). Christians must be taught and committed to Jesus Christ to be powerful against the devil's kingdom.

Chapter Nine

Jesus Cleans His Church

...that he might present it to himself a glorious church, not having spot, or wrinkle, or any such thing; but that it should be holy and without blemish. (Ephesians 5:27)

DELIVERANCE

The subject of casting out demons does not exist in many churches because they have turned away from the topic of deliverance. Some claim that by talking about the devil, we give him glory, while others are simply afraid of the subject. Still others don't believe in evil spirits or in a personal Satan for that matter. Most speak largely out of ignorance and fear.

My testimony of my deliverance happened by the sovereign power of Jesus! This book attempts to dispel unnecessary fear of demons. I believe that my testimonial will help the Christian church to understand the need for using deliverance, as Jesus did, and to help to create a simple pattern that most Christians can follow. Therefore, I am busy writing another teaching book concerning my knowledge and experience of the deliverance ministry. Therefore, in the near future, I will present a broader spectrum of the subject matter. I believe that the power of casting out demons is not new to the church—just forgotten. It is my prayer that the Holy Spirit will lead the pastors into the truth. Love, humility, and truth will always be our standard and goal, but we must go beyond the foundational principles of Christianity into the perfection in Jesus Christ.

BISHOP VAGALAS TESTIFIES

God is restoring deliverance to the body of Christ today. So the Church must have knowledge of deliverance and spiritual warfare. When Jesus called me, He told me to go and testify of what He had spiritually done for me. He cleansed me from the filthiness of the devil. Over time, He taught me to deliver others who were caught in his bondage. I tell you that Jesus wants to clean His Church from false prophets and false doctrines. Because we are living in the last days, there are many that are departing from the truth.

The Bible clearly explains the matter that man will depart from the faith and follow after seducing spirits and doctrines of devils (1 Timothy 4:1-2).

It took more than two years to complete my deliverance. You might wonder why it took so long for my complete deliverance. I can say that partly it was due to the lack of knowledge of the Christian workers. This happened because of Satan's ability to keep the power of the deliverance ministry in the dark. Until recently, you may be surprised that even in my country, as in America, this powerful ministry was not encouraged. Because of the suppression of true deliverance ministers, regrettably they do not enjoy the acceptance and protection of the prayer power of the church. In the beginning of bringing the deliverance ministry back into the Christian church, only Jesus trained the ministers. Even so, things are changing now. Many ministers are beginning to see that they need this powerful ministry to cleanse their churches. They want to see their people mature. The Lord has prepared me and has used me to train many deliverance workers in my church. Through our Bible School, many have been trained and are building churches. They are setting captives free all over the continent of Africa. To God is the glory!

JESUS CHRIST OR SATAN

There are only two sources for supernatural power—Jesus or Satan. Seeking power beyond the Word of God or Jesus Christ, finds one stepping into the world of the Occult. Sadly, the multitudes are seeking mystical religious hopes and they are searching for spiritual answers to fill a void in their souls. Instead, they will enter a door to demonology from which very few will ever return. Once ensnared by the Devil, peoples' minds, bodies and spirits are totally bound by the powers of darkness.

Since engaging in the occult is very religious, the one and only way out is through the grace of God and the Blood of Jesus Christ! Even so, many ask the question, can a Christian be made subject to this occult power? Many church leaders believe they can! Dabbling in the occult by simply reading books on the black arts can bring much distress and demonic oppression. And one who wishes to learn about these ungodly things should consult only books written by Bible scholars for their information.

The Apostle Paul warned: "Ye cannot drink the cup of the Lord, and the cup of devils: Ye cannot be partakers of the Lord's table, and the table of the devils. Do we provoke the Lord to jealousy? Are we stronger than he?" (1 Corinthians 10:21–22). Christians should never seek service, direction or healing from an occultist or psychic. Any Christian that pursues healing from these demons, will be bewitched and guided by the devils. Many have discovered to their surprise and horror that Satan is the one who is willing to divulge supernatural affairs and give them momentary assistance. Often, too late, they find that the real source of their advice and supernatural ability is demonic. They find that Demonic forces are controlling them. Many are seeking purely doctrines of devils. Also many gimmicks and man-made doctrines have replaced Biblical standards, entered into the church and prevailed, stealing the power of the Word. Let's look at a few issues that recently were called to my attention while I was evangelizing in America. Recently, I heard about a church that had put two washtubs in front of the altar. They'd invite the people to come and stand in the first washtub to leave their infirmities in that tub. Then they were asked them to step into the second tub to be cleansed! Incredible! This is pure witchcraft. Witchcraft is one of the works of the flesh that is listed in Galatians 5:19–21.

Whenever we speak of the "the works of the flesh," we are speaking of the Scripture that says, "Now the works of the flesh are manifest, which are these; Adultery, fornication, uncleanness, lasciviousness [lewd, lustful, unchaste], idolatry, witchcraft, hatred, emulations [jealousies, uncurbed spirit of competition], wrath, strife, competition, wrath, strife, sedition [stirring up of strife], heresies, envying, murders, drunkenness, reveling, and such like; of the which I tell you before, as I have also told you in time past, that they which do such things shall not inherit the kingdom of God" (authors' definitions in brackets). There are other scriptures that relate further works of the flesh: Romans 1:28–32; Ephesians 5:3–6; 1 Corinthians 6:9; 2 Timothy 3:2–5, and Revelation 21:8. Evil spirits will torment Christians that live in the state of the flesh and sin. If a door cracks open, that allows Satan to take a shot at a Christian, and they will find a battle that could be avoided.

Whenever a person dabbles in witchcraft, confusion results, many victims can end up going mad. So, they are sent to the insane asylums and never return to sanity! Make no mistake. All occult powers come from Satan. Whenever one uses occult power, he or she will open a door for the devil to enter into their spirit. Once the door is opened, very few victims ever get it to shut again. Workers are very few. Once the works of the flesh are practiced, the person will usually have demonic strongholds present. Moreover, whether the works of the flesh make a headway beyond the curiosity stage or the person engages in demonic activity will depend on the individual involved. Many times the first stage of the works of the flesh is curiosity. Then the spirit of curiosity leads the person to the initial participation. The individual is charmed and fascinated the Holy Spirit is still present, in the case of Christians, to convict him or her of the wrongdoing. Yet, if the Christian ignores the conviction of the Holy Spirit over a period of time, which varies according to the person and situation, that Christian may be in danger of initiating demonic activity by allowing an open doorway to devils to enter. Christian defense to a demonic invasion is broken down through continual sin.

However, it is the responsibility of Christians to keep their vessels pure and holy before the Lord. Look at Ecclesiastes 10:8: "...and who so breakout an hedge, a serpent shall bite him." In biblical times this had to do with a special kind of hedge that was planted around the house to keep dangerous snakes from coming on the premises. If a break or opening were allowed in the hedge, the possibilities of a snake getting in would be high. In other words, if we leave an opening in our spiritual hedge, the possibilities are high that we will be bitten. However, if we keep our defenses or hedge solidly enclosed through living in holiness, we can live in this snake filled world and never be touched by the evil. The Holy Spirit can keep us free from sin as we yield our vessels to Him. Satan can gain access to you only if you give him your will through concurring with his enticements.

Pray and sincerely seek the Holy Spirit's directions about finding a Bible-based church that will teach you the Word of God. The Bible says, "My people are destroyed for lack of knowledge: because thou hast rejected knowledge, I will also reject thee, that thou shalt is no priest to me: seeing thou hast forgotten the law of thy God, I will also forget thy children" (Hosea 4:6).

AVAILABLE TO THE CHURCH

To deliverance ministers, the question, "can Christians have demons?" is not even worth contemplating. Like other deliverance ministries' experiences with thousands of deliverance sessions, my experiences have left no doubt in my mind that Christians not only can, but also do, have demons. It is true, however, that demons cannot "possess" Christians. Unfortunately, the King James Version of the Bible uses an incorrect word. The correct word in the Greek is "demonization," or having demons. Possession implies total control. Demons cannot possess us, but we can possess demons. Theological arguments must give way to experience. Even scientists are known to abandon pet theories when actual experience does not support them. More than 99 percent of the people that I have delivered have been born-again Christians, including many pastors. If a Christian does not believe that Christians can have demons, I suggest that they attend some deliverance sessions. If it is possible that demons can reside in the human body, they need to be cast out!

When Jesus began His ministry, He delivered many people who were tormented by demons. He also accomplished many of His healings by casting out the spirit of infirmity: Matthew 4:24; 8:16, 28; 9:33; 12:22; 15:22; Mark 1:27; 3:11; 5:13; 7:26; Luke 4:33, 36; 6:18; 7:21; 8:2; 10:20; 11:14.

The deliverance ministry is as controversial today as it was when Jesus walked on the earth. Notice how the religious people of His day charged, "He cast out devils by Beelzebub" (Luke 11:13). These people were claiming that Jesus was casting out devils by the power of Beelzebub, the lord of the flies. Jesus had so much compassion for the slaves of Satan that He rose above the slanderous peer pressure to free the captives. To sum up, Satan's strategy in His day, as well as this day, is to lead people to doubt the reality of Jesus and His power.

DESTROYING THEIR PAST

When a person is saved, I have found that his past must be destroyed. The demons that controlled him must be driven out. Then the person can live for Jesus. There is tremendous power in the Word of God that is available to His people to free the captives. If people have demons, then the church must give them the opportunity to be delivered! So, the Church must awaken to the Word of God and get back to the basics. For instance, the Bible says, "The Spirit of the Lord is upon me, because he hath anointed me to preach the gospel to the poor; he hath sent me to heal the brokenhearted, to preach deliverance to the captives and recovering of sight to the blind, to set at liberty them that are bruised" (Luke 4:18).

The Word also reveals the empowerment of his servant "For this purpose the Son of God was manifested, that he might destroy the works of the devil" (1 John 3:8).

Jesus taught me His Word. He showed me in the Scriptures where he had defeated the devils. Then He told me that I could do the same things that the ministers had done for me. When I first began to minister, I'd go into the streets and tell people about Jesus. He would anoint me and many people started getting free—right there on the streets of Ghana! Oh how wonderful those days were. Every day was a new exciting experience with my new Savior. He has taught me the deliverance ministry. The Kingdom of God had arrived in many lives. I knew my destiny was to live for Jesus and touch the people. Before my conversion to Jesus, I was like Adam, lost; but now I am happily found. I have been blessed to discover the truth of Jesus Christ. The same as Adam who was trapped, alone, afraid, in a world he never made, I too was enslaved and under his bondage. Satan had brought corruption, disease and poverty into the world. Therefore, the bondage of sin and its consequences create alienation from one's fellow man and to God.

POWER FROM JESUS

Then Jesus came and said, "I am the way, the truth, and the life" (John 14:6). Man's own unaided efforts to solve his problems through intellectual, economic, political, social or psychological skills are soon to fail. "Neither is there salvation in any other: for there is none other name under heaven given among men, whereby we must be saved" (Acts 4:12). Salvation is a free gift from God. It is a work of God in which He rescues man from eternal ruin. The Bible says, "Whosoever shall call on the Name of the Lord shall be delivered" (Joel 2:32). The condition for successful deliverance from demons is absolute honesty. In like manner, it is a willingness to turn from and confess all known sin, renunciation of all contact with evil spirits, and forgiving all people.

Freedom comes with a complete surrender in every area of a person's life to the Lordship of Jesus Christ. The New Testament Church made devils tremble and the Bible said that they turned the world upside down. Her ministers drove out legions of demons. Likewise, they had faith and power to open prison doors, heal the sick, and convert. Today, people are ensnared by witchcraft, pornography, false religions, etc. Many churches are filled with dull ritualism and materialisms. They have lost the knowledge of God's power. They are going to need the same anointing as the early Church had in order to bring the masses to Christ. It is time to toss aside all teachings that dismiss God's supernatural power to bring people into the fullness of Jesus Christ.

Hopefully my testimony of deliverance will serve to bring needed attention to the reality of the power of demonic infestation and God's power of the deliverance ministry to free captives. That is, the gift of discerning of spirits is so desperately required to release spiritual captives in the same manner that Jesus Christ did. Remember, if the apostle Paul preached and taught without signs and wonders following, his message would not have had its full impact. In truth, it would not have been the gospel fully preached! He said to the Corinthians, "Truly, the signs of an apostle were wrought among you in all patience, in signs, and wonders, and mighty deeds," (2 Corinthians 12:12).

OCCULT EXPLOSION

The reason that the Church needs to restore the power of the deliverance ministry is the fact that the witchcraft power is rising worldwide. Astrologers, numerologists, New Age channelers, palm readers, and other so-called seers are making millions of dollars playing the "game." They will try to plot your destiny or attempt to advise you on any matter for a handsome fee. Some will predict the outcome of the next presidential election or tell of the exact date the world will end! "And every spirit that confesseth not that Jesus Christ is come in the flesh is not of God: and this is that spirit of Antichrist, whereof ye have heard that it should come; and even now already is it in the world" (1 John 4:3).

Why are housewives, business executives and large numbers of Americans becoming so obsessed with the darkness of the occult? Is it really "just for kicks" as some suggest, or is there a terrible fear of the future and what is "beyond?" How does it all begin? What are the results? "Be not deceived; God is not mocked: for whatsoever a man soweth, that shall he also reap" (Galatians 6:7).

The word occult is defined as hidden knowledge or wisdom beyond human understanding. It could also be described as getting supernatural perceptual experience from sources other than God. "The secret things (hidden knowledge) belong to the Lord our God: but those things which are revealed belong unto us, and to our children forever, that we may do all the words of this law" (Deuteronomy 29:29).

One young girl said, "I was bored and unhappy. Then someone told me that I had telepathic powers. That person gave me some occult books. I became fascinated with ESP, witchcraft, and the like. I wanted power to change my life. It wasn't long until I was hooked. I wanted more power. It's hungry and the more you discover, the more it takes over your mind and soul. But when I got it, I was terrified. Great confusion comes. I almost lost my mind before I found release through Jesus Christ."

If Jesus does not really occupy the highest place in our hearts, controlling all, something else will—millions are now serving other gods. "For thou shalt worship no other god: for the Lord, whose name is Jealous, is a jealous God" (Exodus 34:14).

THE OCCULT IS RELIGIOUS

The modernistic occult movement is a do-it-yourself religion. It is not based on right and wrong. People can do any evil thing that they desire and still have mystical experiences. People are looking for a power or force other than the just-living God. They are seeking a supernatural experience that will require no change in their sin life. They want supernatural adventure without spiritual responsibility. Others participate in the occult through curiosity and knowing better. Even if a person does not know the demon power behind these activities and does not believe in them, they are still sinful, they will have supernatural results over their lives. There is no such thing as innocent participation nor can you study occult materials to disprove them.

Interest in the occult is idolatry and is a clear violation of the First Commandment (Exodus 20:3–5). As the Bible warns, idolatry is "fellowship with devils and provokes the Lord to Jealousy" (1 Corinthians 10:20–22).

Seeking help from the occult is the same as calling upon another god. It is insulting to God who made heaven and earth to consult with a demonically inspired person for spiritual guidance and to participate is an abomination to God and will bring His swift judgment upon the person and also their descendants. "Thou shalt have no other gods before me. Thou shalt not bow down thyself unto them, nor serve them: for I thy God am a jealous God, visiting the iniquity of the fathers upon the children unto the third and fourth generation them that hate me" (Deuteronomy 5: 7–9).

Christians must never seek help, guidance or healing from an occultist or psychic. If any Christian seeks healing from these demons, they will be lured and led by the devils. Many have discovered to their shock and terror that Satan is the one who is willing to disclose supernatural things to give temporary help. Often too late, they find that the real source of their guidance and supernatural power is demonic. They become confused, unable to pray, read their Bible and uninterested in Christian activity. They drop away from the Church. Many fall away from the Faith never to return. "Now the Spirit speaketh expressly that in the latter times some shall depart from the faith, giving heed to seducing spirits, and doctrines of devils" (1 Timothy 4:1).

Once a person knows God and turns away, Satan is always there to give them a false prophet or a false religious experience. Unfortunately, help is rare once a person is entrapped. The workers are truly few and most churches are totally ignorant concerning the power they have in Jesus' name to set the captives free. The Scriptures prophesied of increased occult activity and some will leave the faith and follow seducing spirits, and doctrines of demons. God's word clearly gives us views of the graphic occult practices that He defines as abominations. Christians and Jews will surely be without excuse when they stand before the Judgment seat of God because they have the Word of God, but do not believe it.

"When thou art come into the land which the Lord thy God giveth thee, thou shalt not learn to do after the abominations of those nations. There shall not be found among you any one that maketh his son or daughter to pass through the fire or that useth divination, or an observer of times, or an enchanter, or a witch, or a charmer, or a consulter with familiar spirits, or a wizard, or a necromancer. For all that do these things are an abomination unto the Lord: and because of these abominations the Lord thy God doth drive them out from before thee," (Deuteronomy 18:9–12).

The occult according to the Bible was shown to Moses and Aaron in Pharaoh's courts. They witnessed that the devil's priest could copy their powers (Exodus 7), but God's power was greater. Aaron's rod swallowed up the magicians' rods. Any spiritual power is greater than any human power and many people today need the greater power of Jesus to free them from the devil's powers. Occult powers come from Satan. When one uses occult power, he or she opens a door for the devil to come into their lives. The Bible talks about demons. The King James Version of the Bible calls them devils.

WARNING FROM EXPERIENCE

Children of the world, I warn you to stay away from occult-witchcraft television programs, such as *Sabrina, the Teenage Witch, Buffy the Vampire Slayer, True Calling, Angels, Crossing Over,* and *Charmed.* Movies are also designed to draw you into the powers of darkness. There are movies such as *The Craft, Practical Magic, The Rainbow and the Serpent,* and books such as *Teen Witch* and *The*

Little Book of Hexes for Women. Remember to stay away from the Harry Potter books and occult-based cartoons and the many devices that are being produced to steal your souls. These materials have made the once forbidden occult both fashionable and fun across the United States and overseas. The powers of the Devil are real and they will quickly capture you and enslave your souls. They will mark you for hell and you may never be free again.

HIGHWAY TO FREEDOM

Since I had past experience of working with these demons, Jesus specifically called me to expose demonic activity. He told me to teach the Christian Church how to defeat them. The Bible says, "My people are destroyed for lack of knowledge: because thou hast rejected knowledge, I will also reject thee, that thou shall be no priest to me: seeing thou hast forgotten the law of thy God, I will also forget thy children" (Hosea 4:6).

In Africa, when a person gets saved, we take them away for deliverance. We immediately work to destroy their past. We labor to deliver them from the devils that have guided their lives for years.

It has been my experience that once demons gain entrance to a human body, they are able to establish various strongholds. They are invited into a person but they must be kicked out. To illustrate, a demonic stronghold could be called a spirit of infirmity. This could cause such a victim to be constantly sick and eventually become terminally or drastically ill with many ailments. Another stronghold could cause spirits such as, unforgiveness, rebellion, fear, (these names usually correspond to their functions of jobs) to operate in the same person. The chain of command controls all strongholds and demons can act inside a person's body. These are called ruling spirits. The minister must bind the strongman.

If the minister should fail to do so, then the demons that are being cast out will draw strength and reinforcement from the strongman that resides in the person. However, all the strongholds ultimately take their orders from the strongman (Principalities) in the heavens. A deliverance minister must destroy the stronghold (Principalities) by binding (tying up or not permitting) the power of the strongman. The minister must cut and cast off all cords between the strongman and the spirits that reside inside the person. Then the minister should continue the deliverance. If the minister fails to cut these cords that connect ruling spirits in the heavens, then the spirit that is being cast out will draw strength and reinforcement from the strongman. They are residing as clusters or nests of spirits that are connected to the stronghold (Principalities). These demons dwell flocked together, such as anger, murder, violence, hostility, unforgiveness, perversion, homosexuality and other demons inside people.

Chapter Ten

New Ministries

In some countries, whenever celebrities are saved, they are immediately elevated to the pulpits of Christian church. However, before we allow anyone to minister, the person must be submitted to the church leadership and be under us for many years. (Bishop Vagalas Kanco)

JOIN A SPIRITUAL CHURCH

After I got born again, I went through deliverance for two years because my demons were very strong. I sat under my pastor for five or six years. The church must make sure that you won't come and cause a mess. In Africa, we don't allow you to get born again today and tomorrow let you preach. We don't look at your zeal, how you love the Lord and immediately push you to go and preach. No, no, no, no, we won't even let you go to a visitation, because you can fall into trouble. We must witness you aligning yourself with the leadership of the church. You must go through training and study under us for several years. We must see your spiritual growth to testify that now you have grown. You can handle spiritual power. I hope the church will take this advice, because we are on a battlefield. Please understand that if your people are not fully prepared, they can be wounded. People are often wounded and destroyed. In Africa, we don't play games with the Devil. In Africa, the devils kill!

Believe me. It is not just a matter of saying Jesus loves' you. Let me tell you a real story. Recently, I had about ten Dutch missionaries that were visiting us from Holland. When they came to our city, they went to one of the idolatrous villages. In this particular village, you can trust that demonic powers will be there. In the case of these Dutchmen, the people that they were talking to were the very people that take care of the shrine. These Dutchmen were not spiritually prepared for what they were facing. They did not have spiritual discernment. Truthfully, the natives started casting voodoo spirits upon these people. When they left and returned to our city, they started removing their pants because the demons of insanity had possessed them. The demon in charge of madness is very powerful. He is so strong. In Africa the wizards release spirits of madness. In fact, the person that doesn't know anything about deliverance and demonology, the spirit of madness will grab the person.

Once this happens, this person will become totally helpless unless a deliverance minister is called. The demons that had possessed the Dutchmen were overpowering. So when they started removing their pants, the police were able to overcome them. I was in my office that day when they called me, "You will have to come to the police station."

"Why?" I asked.

"You will have to come," the policeman responded. "We need you, immediately. We have some Christian Dutchmen at the police station that have gone stark raving mad."

Immediately I rushed over to the police station and found the policemen trying to talk to these Dutchmen. Moreover, some of them were dancing about in hysteria. It was pandemonium at the station and truly dangerous.

Thank God that the policeman was a Christian. "Truthfully, people who are not trained in spiritual warfare and demonology cannot minister to them," said the police chief.

I began to pray and do spiritual warfare. As I bound the powers of the devils, the Dutchmen began to calm down. Then, I asked them what had happened. They told me that they had gone to the demonic village. After subduing these powers of darkness, I knew that they had to be filled with the Holy Spirit.

"My God, my God," I replied, "We have to empower them. Give them some injections to calm them down. Then you must bring them to my church and we will cast every spirit out."

In Africa, a minister must know certain things. In America, spirits are milder than the ones in Africa.

You pamper them in your country, saying something like this, "Oh, it's going to be all right, ha, ha." But in Africa, the demons are strong and aggressive. We know that we must drive them out or it's all over for the person. Believe me, in my country, devils kill!

DESTROY THEIR PAST

If you ever see someone receiving deliverance, it will really help you to believe. When Annaias laid his hands on Paul, his scales fell from his eyes. The scales were his past. Paul needed cleansing, and demons had been driven out through the power of God. After salvation, there is a need for deliverance.

When people get saved in our church, we take them through a lot of deliverance. Soon we destroy their past and only then, they have a real chance of serving Jesus.

In (Luke 13), the Scripture declares that Satan can bind people. Demons can cause: dumbness (Matthew 9:32–33), blindness (Matthew 12:22), insanity (Luke 8:26–35), suicidal mania (Mark 9:22), personal injuries (Mark 9:18), inflict physical defects and deformities (Luke 13:11-17). Once they get control over a human body they can come and go at will (Luke 11:24–26). There are three stages of influence: temptation (James 1:12), torment, (Hebrews 12:15), and control (Acts 5:3), which is possession.

The Lord is training an army to work in the harvest fields. Jesus Christ, as presented by the Father and also Jesus' testimony, is according to the Word, "And Jesus came and spake unto them, saying, All power is given to me in heaven and in earth" (Matthew 28:18).

He is revealed as Deity with absolute sovereignty and authority over the universe for eternity. This includes all the power of the enemy! In the midst of all the disagreements of His time, Jesus' disciples also wrestled to understand what his identity meant for their lives. In fact, they also struggled with the question of his Deity. Even after many experiences of Jesus' power, the disciples had difficulty in every new situation simply trusting in God's abundant love. They even questioned the power to provide for them through Jesus. In particular, they were beginning to see some things about their master, but they have not yet conceived the meaning of his miraculous feeding of the five thousand people. When Jesus asked them about popular opinions of his identity, they reported the rumors that he was John the Baptist or one of the ancient prophets. Jesus centered upon them, "But who do you say that I am?" Jesus insisted. Then, when Peter spoke for them, he revealed that Jesus was the Messiah, the "Son of the living God." Jesus blessed him for making that confession and gave the revelation of the foundation of His church.

"You are Peter [Petros]" meaning little rock, Jesus said in a play on words, "and on this rock [Petra]" meaning large rock, "I will build my church" (Matthew 16:18).

Jesus was telling Peter that He was building His Church upon the foundation of Himself and His testimony.

CHRISTIAN AUTHORITY

The Apostle Paul thanks the Father who delivered us from the power of darkness and translated us into the kingdom of his dear Son (Colossians 1:13). He describes Christ's sovereignty in a passage that celebrates Christ as the Creator of the universe, supreme over every creature. "For by him were all things created, that are in heaven, and that are in earth, visible and invisible, whether they be thrones, or dominions, or principalities, or powers: all things were created by him and for him" (Colossians 1:16). He is the head of his body, the church, and the first to conquer death. Although in Christ, "all the fullness" of God was pleased to dwell, Paul asserts, it was ultimately only by his human suffering and through "the blood of His cross, by him to reconcile all things" to God and make peace. Jesus Christ is Lord, and we worship Him in the Spirit of truth (John 8:32).

God created the Church and the foundation of it is built upon the work and Person of Jesus Christ. The Lord told me to tell His people that He is able to back up His Word if Christians would use their authority. I asked Jesus why the Church seems, at times, to be so defeated? He showed me that if His people will return to the basics of His Word use it coupled together with their authority, demons must obey! They don't have a choice. In other words, demons tremble and run when we walk, talk and agree with Word of God. However, many people are not using their authority to overcome the powers of darkness.

DELIVERANCE IS FOR TODAY

When Jesus called me, He sent me to go and tell His church my testimony. He set me free and trained me to set the captives free just as He did when He ministered on the earth. In like manner, He taught me through His Word exactly how to minister to clean people spiritually. As a result, by His anointing and through the power of His name, I ministered miracles, healing and deliverance. He told me that I could cast the demons out in His name, "And these signs shall follow them that believe; In my name shall they cast out devils; they shall speak with new tongues" (Mark 16:17).

I knew the importance of deliverance, because of my freedom. Trust me, thousands have been set free over the years because I believed His Word. Over and over, I've seen believers delivered from the power of Satan and His demons. Jesus' power works every time! Indeed, while I believe that experience is not the basis for the interpretation of the Bible, I've read many Christian writers who agree with me that Christians do experience demon influence.

For instance, Dr. Merrill Unger writes the following: "In demon influence, evil spirits exert power over a person short of actual possession. Such influence may vary from mild harassment to extreme subjection when body and mind become dominated and held in slavery to spirit agents."

He goes on to say, "Christians, as well as non-Christians can be so influenced. They may be oppressed, vexed, depressed, hindered and bound by demons."

Unger is frank to say that he had written in 1952, "To demon possession, only unbelievers are exposed."

Then 20 years later Unger said, "This statement was inferred, since Scripture does not clearly settle the question. It was based on the assumption that an evil spirit could not indwell the redeemed body together with the Holy Spirit." He wrote that missionaries from all over the world wrote to him telling of cases to the contrary and as the author notes, the claims of the missionaries "appear valid."

There are still those among us who would disagree that there is an unseen invisible force in the world. They believe in only what they can see with their eyes, touch with their hands, hear with their ears and feel with their body. The Bible clearly teaches that there are two supernatural personalities that are contending for the souls of men—the spirit of God or the spirit of Satan. There is no neutral middle ground. We serve God or the Devil.

Evangelizing in America

When I evangelize in America, I've noticed that many in the Christian churches do not believe in the need for deliverance ministers. However, through the gift of discerning of spirits, I can see the need. Ignoring the invasion of evil demons will not solve problems. It will only bring spiritual blindness and give demons more open courses to work the powers of darkness. Failure to recognize Satan's power and the work of his demons can be a fatal mistake to the church. The Devil's greatest weapon is pretending not to exist. Demons, in their constant harassment activity, overcome and occupy when there is yielding of the mind to them. Their primary purpose is to draw their captives first away from the reality of Jesus Christ's blood atonement and then, down into the pit of hell.

There is much bondage, when people overlook the reality of the power of deliverance from evil spirits. It is my understanding that most seminaries in America never teach the doctrine of deliverance. Although there is widespread occult revival of witchcraft and psychic phenomena being spread through movies, television, magazines and other sources, most ministers have never been called upon to deal with someone who is under the influence of an evil spirit. Many believe that evil spirits are found only in Africa or some other remote regions in the world but they are also found in America! In the western part of the world, demon activity is considered to be something alien. Actually, they have renamed them as other things, such as sickness, depression, worry, fear, etc. So they remain hidden as something other than demons and they can be counseled or drugged away.

The truth is that in a large part of the world, demons are a part of the people's everyday life. They worship the demons and believe that these demons have power to give them a good life or a bad one. Eyewitnesses today are too numerous to bypass the evidences of demonology and their ability to possess human beings. Seeing captives free from demonic bondages are the best arguments.

Jesus told me, "I have sent you to teach about these demons because you know them."

That is, I understand how they work in the affairs of people. Besides, I have witnessed the results of their work in the lives of people in Africa. As a former witch doctor, I saw the destruction of many people by the powers of darkness. As a Christian evangelist, I can see the spiritual blindness of the people in the world. The Lord told me, "Go and tell them."

Satan is a strong spiritual being that is a master of deceptio-n, able to hide his existence from many today. He likes it that way because they don't know how to resist him. We are truly engaged in spiritual warfare. A daily walk with Jesus Christ means, "putting on the whole armor of God." When Satan attempts to attack, we must resist the devil and he will flee from us (James 4:7).

The Apostle Paul reveals that we wrestle against powers, rulers of darkness of this world, and spiritual wickedness in high places (Ephesians 6:12). God gave us a part in the defeat of these evil forces. We are to "Pull down the strongholds and stand against the wiles of the Devil" (2 Corinthians 10:4).

The Bible never told us to ignore the Devil. Again and again Jesus cast out demons, even engaging them in conversations. He taught His disciples to cast out demons in His name. Jesus definitely believed in casting out demons and they practiced it. To sum up, the ministry of casting out demons is not some spooky hocus Pocus exercise. Authority to cast demons out is life and freedom. It's the Kingdom of God coming upon the person. It is the power of God!

SPIRITS OF DECEPTION

The Lord revealed to me that part of the problem is that the spirits of deception are freely working in many of His Churches. Regrettably, many Christians believe that they do not have to know anything concerning the evil deceptions of demons. The Apostle John warns (in 2 John 7) "For many deceivers are entered into the world, who confess not that Jesus Christ is come in the flesh. This is a deceiver and an Antichrist."

When Christians are sleeping, the devils freely work. The kingdom of the Antichrist has been trying to come into existence since Jesus Christ died on the Cross.

Jesus told his disciples, "Occupy till I come" (Luke 19:13).

Satan uses demonic spirits to bring his power to the earth. Author and deliverance minister Derek Prince underscores this vital point that I am trying to make. He reveals this truth when he writes:

> Today, by divine manifestation of God's foresight care for His creatures, the veils of convention and carnality are once again being drawn aside, and the church of Jesus Christ is being confronted by the same manifest opposition of demon power that confronted the church of the New Testament. In these circumstances, the church must once again explore the resources of authority and power made available to her through the truth of the Scripture, the anointing of the Holy Spirit, and the Name and the Blood of the Lord Jesus Christ.

The Bible clearly shows us that we are not wrestling against the Father, Son and the Holy Spirit but against Satan and his forces of evil.

Author Jesse Penn-Lewis defines the satanic forces described in Ephesians 6:12, as: "Principalities - force and dominion dealing with nations and governments; Powers - having authority and power of action in all the spheres open to them; World Rulers - governing the darkness and blindness of the world at large; wicked Spirits in heavenly places. The forces are being directed in and upon the Church of Jesus Christ in wiles, fiery darts, onslaught, and every conceivable deception about doctrine which they are capable of planning." †

† Jesse Penn-Lewis, *The War on the Saints* (Thomas E. Lowe, Ltd., 1973).

Chapter Eleven

Power of Jesus

Satan has a special Interest in the Church of Jesus Christ. We can well believe that he will do everything in his power to sidetrack, hinder, weaken, and destroy the church's ministry.‡

HIS GRACE IS SUFFICIENT

Jesus told me to teach His Church concerning Satan's kingdom and the weakness of his demons. He said that His grace and power are sufficient.

"Tell My people that they must return to the basics of the Bible. Tell them that I left them My name. If they will use My name, they will be victorious. Demons are real, but so am I!"

Many Christian writers have confirmed the reality of demonology such as the Lord told me.

Just as God gave the people of Israel the promise and then told them to take it by force, the Apostle Paul gave the Church the revelation knowledge of the powers and principalities in Ephesians 6. He disclosed that the church was in spiritual warfare. He gave us the keys too win the battle by using our spiritual weapons.

Jesus Christ told us in Matthew 11:12: "The kingdom of heaven suffereth violence and the violent take it by force."

The Church of Jesus Christ should make the difference in every community. Jesus' saints are His instruments on earth to bring His kingdom upon the earth. The Church has His power because He is

‡ Frank and Ida Mae Hammond, *Pigs in the Parlor: A Practical Guide to Deliverance* (Impact Christian Books, Inc., 1973).

sitting at the right hand of God waiting and willing to give us the power too win every spiritual battle.

He also provided spiritual weapons. Our weapons consist of using His name, His blood, His Word, His power and prayer. The Apostle Paul shows this transference of His power to us who believe (Ephesians 1:19–22): "And what is the exceeding greatness of his power to us-ward who believe, according to the working of his mighty power, which he wrought in Christ, when he raised him from the dead and set him at His own right hand in the heavenly places, Far above all principality and power and might, and dominion, and every name that is named, not only in this world, but also in that which is to come: And hath put all things under his feet, and gave him to be the head over all things to the church."

If I've learned anything as a Christian, it is that Jesus Christ has superior knowledge and power. To be sure I'd be dead if this were not true. He has always proved His Word and power to me. I've been victorious every time.

The problem is, some Saints never understand their position in Jesus Christ. Too often Christians are prone to be skeptical about the existence of demons. But they are real. They are responsible to Satan for deceiving curious humans. Satan taught me when I was in witchcraft that nations were turning and seeking after other gods. Today I know it's true as I write, there are covens worldwide.

Sadly, only a few people are able to escape the clutches of the Devil. Whenever one steps through the doorways to darkness, powerful demons capture and keep them under slavery and total dominion. In fact, the victim cannot be freed unless a caring Christian prays for his or her release. Sadly, many Christians have also fallen under these powers due to their spiritual ignorance of the Word of God. Regrettably, many strange doctrines have arrived in some churches.

DISCERNING SPRITS

The Bible warns us to be very careful in our choice of spiritual experiences. The segregation of ourselves from receiving unscriptural false teachings will protect us. By separation, we are shielded from receiving the evil spirits that are motivating the false prophet or false teacher, from entering into our spirit.

John 4:3: “Beloved, believe not every spirit, but try the spirits whether they are of God, because many false prophets are gone out into the world. Hereby know ye the Spirit of God. Every spirit that confesseth not that Jesus Christ is come in the flesh is not of God; and this is that spirit of Antichrist, whereof ye have heard that it should come; and even now already is it in the world. They are of the world; therefore, speak they of the world, and the world heareth them.”

You must guard your words and then words that spoken through others have power to transfer evil spirits. This is why you should carefully watch what you hear. If you allow yourself to listen to a minister that mixes the Word of God with anything, you will become cold and hard of hearing the Word.

The Apostle Paul wrote with a grieved heart to the Galatian Church that he had lovingly labored with the Gospel of the Lord Jesus Christ: “O foolish Galatians, who hath bewitched you, that ye should not obey the truth, before whose eyes Jesus Christ hath been ‘evidently set forth, crucified among you” (Galatians 3:1).

The Apostle Paul inquired, “Who had bewitched the believers to draw them away from the truth?” Effects upon them were not just the effects of wrong mental impressions conveyed by false teachers but were the effects of evil spirits imposing false doctrine through false teachers. Reference does not suggest that believers enjoy an easy exemption from the activities of devils but are particularly targeted by them.

In 1 Timothy 4:1–2, how wicked spirits attack the spiritual believer by deception and beguile him away from the faith through the use of false prophets. Most believers have adopted the mistaken idea that if they ignore Satan, he will ignore them. Scripturally, such a position is indefensible. (1 Peter, 5:8–9; James 4:7; 2 Corinthians 2:11).

GOD WANTS A DIFFERENCE

In the Book of Leviticus God institutes a difference between the clean and the unclean and God has a distinct purpose for this difference. The primary reason is that in the world we find two spirits. Notice there are two battle lines. There are two persons who are deadly enemies. These two are God and Satan. To sum up, all the forces have one goal. Their mission is to reach the souls of men with their message. The outcome of this battle will save or damn that soul eternally. Hence, so that the message of salvation will be a clear signal, God wants a difference between His people and the people of the world.

The absence of teaching a difference is in many circumstances one of the greatest causes of confusion in the world. Furthermore, those who should be the benefactors of the Gospel seem more confused by the lack of difference than if they had never heard the message. The prophet Ezekiel lamented this point in chapter 22:26, and then later, in chapter 44:23, Ezekiel said, "Men should be taught the difference."

As surely as there is a difference between light and darkness and righteousness and unrighteousness, there is a difference between the Christian and the unsaved person. In 1 Peter 2:9, we see that the people of God are special in comparison to the people of the world. God's people are a chosen people, made royal and holy and called out of the worldly atmosphere of ungodliness.

Spiritual security comes by carefully watching where you go. If you find yourself in the wrong place, then respond by using your spiritual weapons for divine protection. You must bind the devils according to Matthew 18:18, and place yourself under Jesus' blood. This is the reason that a person has to choose the places they attend and their friendships very carefully. When choosing spiritual fellowship, it is important to seek the approval of the Holy Spirit. It is also very necessary to seek a biblically based church that is teaching the truth of God's Word. Bible believing churches will encourage spiritual growth and sanctification. These types of churches will emphasize building Christian character and bringing a person into a relationship with Jesus. Jesus must be the central issue of the Gospel. Many will teach about "God," not featuring Jesus. He must be revealed as the Lord of Lords as the only pathway back to God!

TESTING SPIRITS

Is it unloving to "test the spirits?" It is imperative that Christians know exactly what they believe and why they believe it. Indeed, Satan's greatest objective is to deceive, as Jesus warned, that he would try to deceive even the elect (His people), (Matthew 24:24). Also in the second epistle of Peter, we read: "But there were false prophets also among the people, even as there shall be false teachers among you, who privily shall bring in damnable heresies, even denying the Lord that bought them and bring upon themselves swift destruction. And many shall follow their pernicious ways; by reason of whom the way of truth shall be evil spoken of. And through covetousness shall they with feigned words make merchandise of you: whose judgment now of a long time lingereth not, and their damnation slumbereth not." (2 Peter 2:1–3).

The Word of God explicitly warns that just prior to the return of Jesus Christ, a great apostasy, or "falling away" from the true Gospel, will occur on an unprecedented scale with the Christian Church. Jesus also prophesied that many false prophets, such as those that plagued the Israelite nation would arise, men commissioned by Satan himself to seduce the unwary into the worship of false gods.

These deceivers, as we have already seen, will not only look like true believers, but even the message they bring will superficially sound like that of the Bible. And yet, as the Apostle Paul stated so clearly in (2 Corinthians 11:4), theirs is a different Jesus, a different gospel and a different spirit.

As the Bible says, "The Spirit of the Lord (Jehovah) is upon me; because (Jehovah) hath anointed me to preach good tiding unto the meek; he hath sent me to bind up the brokenhearted, to proclaim liberty to the captives, and the opening of the prison to them that are bound; to proclaim the year of (Jehovah's) favor, and the day of vengeance of our God; to comfort all that mourn; to appoint unto them that mourn in Zion, to give unto them a garland for ashes, the oil of joy for mourning, the garment of praise for the spirit of heaviness; that they may be called trees of righteousness, the planting of (Jehovah) that he may be glorified!" (Isaiah 61:1–3). The truth is, only the Christian can present the truth that saves, heals, and sets a person free.

Some manifestations can suggest occult bondage by occult demon spirits. However, causation must be used for some of these symptoms may originate from other causes such as, mental confusion, extended periods of gloominess, depression, unpredictable behavior, stealing, sexual lust, perversions, appetites, temper tantrums, uncontrollable hatred or suspicion, jealousy, resentment, delusions, compulsive lying, gambling, obsessive thoughts of self-destruction, blasphemous thoughts against the blood of Christ, God or The Holy Spirit, speech and behavior abnormalities, religious delusion, seeing apparitions, hearing spiritual voices, chronic physical ailments that do not respond to medical treatment and fear of dying.

Release can come only through Confession of Faith in Jesus Christ. Jesus is the only deliverer from the powers of darkness. Confession of Occult involvement and repentance (Godly sorrow) and a merciful God will not abandon His children to Satan. Confession means to agree with God and the Sin. Renounce Satan and command him to depart! It is imperative when a blood pact or agreement has been made with the powers of darkness to renounce all agreements.

A person that has invited Satan in by occult activity must boot him out! It is best that this person asks the Lord to lead him to a Christian to pray with him. Satan may well have pretended to be a gentleman when he entered, but when possessed, that person will have to kick him out like a trespasser to make him leave. He leaves by direct command to Satan himself to depart in the Name of Jesus (not a prayer or request, but a command).

This person must be firm and choose too forever to take back the place that he once gave to him! This new Christian must associate himself with other Christians who will pray and stand with Him. It is most important that he fills himself with the things of God to stay free. This delivered, new Christian can never go back because he will be seven times worse!

CONFESSION OF FAITH IN JESUS CHRIST

Victims of occult dominion must, with all sincerity, trust Christ and confess Him as Savior. Jesus is the only deliverer from the powers of darkness (demons). They must call upon the name of Jesus and be reconciled to God before dealing with the problem of occult involvement. This Christian must be determined because Satan does not let people go easily. It is only through the blood of Christ and if a person is open and honest in the confession of Jesus as Savior and Lord, that release will come.

CONFESSION—OCCULT INVOLVEMENT

The afflicted person must make the decision to change his or her ways. By confessing the specific sins of occult transgression, the enemy is unmasked. The enemy is exposed. The strategy by which the person was held in bondage is broken. When a person confesses this evil, it means to agree with God about the sin.

RENOUNCE SATAN

Satan has a right to enter anytime a pact or agreement has been concluded with the powers of darkness. This is because the person has opened the door for him. But such activities granted to Satan give access through occult involvement. It is important that all agreements must be annulled. These spiritual contracts can only be dissolved by a conscious verbal act of repudiation on the part of the one that is subjected. The minister can say. "You must depart in the Name of Jesus," (Not a prayer request, but a command). Let me make it clear once and forever, the victim and the minister will take back the place, the agreement, the lease, and the pact that was given to Satan.

TO BE FREE

Accordingly the person must realize that deliverance is a walk, as well as experience. The delivered person must safeguard the ground taken from Satan for Jesus. After deliverance, it is necessary to walk in the will of God according to the Word of God. They must be biblically taught. They must throw away all occult objects, charms and literature. This is essential to a sustained freedom. All occult objects and idolatries are to be done away with and destroyed (Acts 19:18,19). "Put on the whole armor of God that you may be able you stand against the wiles of the devil" (Ephesians 6:11). Remember this: without Jesus Christ a person has no life, no peace (Romans 3:17); all are death without Him. There is no excuse because God's Word is too plain (Romans 1:20). There truly is no escape, neglecting Him will send a poor soul to hell (2 Peter 3:9).

I will advise the victim, as my pastor told me, after salvation and deliverance, "You can stay free!"

The most reliable insurance policy against demonic oppression, is to be saved and filled with the Holy Spirit and living for Jesus and resistance by holy living. God gives us an impenetrable armor as is shown in Ephesians 6:10-17. Here is also great power in using the blood of Jesus in the presence of the Devil. He will try to come back and attack the new Christian's flesh, mind, and spirit. The person can simply rebuke him in the powerful name of Jesus. Remind him of his defeat by the fact of the living Jesus Christ Who is in all born-again Christians covered by the blood of Jesus. Tell him that he no longer owns the deed to your soul. Command him to go in the name of Jesus. Devils no longer live in your body because you are now filled with the Holy Spirit and by the power of the name of Jesus; the person is freed from the powers of darkness.

You can be free and stay free in the name of Jesus!

Made in the USA
Lexington, KY
21 July 2012